The MUIR WOODS HANDBOOK

An Insider's Guide to the Park

As related by Ranger Mia

By Susan and Phil Frank

Pomegranate

SAN FRANCISCO

Published by Pomegranate Communications, Inc.
Box 6099, Rohnert Park, California 94927
www.pomegranate.com

Pomegranate Europe Ltd.
Fullbridge House, Fullbridge
Maldon, Essex CM9 4LE, England

Muir Woods is a wonder of nature, and it is in the nature of nature to be in constant flux. Sometimes change happens over eons, but it can be rapid and unpredictable. For this reason, although we have made our very best efforts to provide the most up-to-date information possible as of press time, we can't guarantee the accuracy or completeness of this book's contents. The publisher and author assume no legal responsibility for the effects of inclusion or exclusion of any premises or services, commercial or otherwise, from this book. The names of businesses herein are provided as a service to readers and not as a recommendation or guarantee.

Library of Congress Cataloging-in-Publication Data

Frank, Susan, 1948–
        The Muir Woods handbook : an insider's guide to the park, as related by Ranger Mia / by Susan and Phil Frank.
          p. cm.
        Includes bibliographical references and index.
        ISBN 0-7649-1027-2 (pbk.)
        1. Muir Woods National Monument (Calif.) Guidebooks.
I. Frank, Phil. II. Title.
F868.M3F73 1999
917.94'62—dc21   99-15328
                                                 CIP

Pomegranate Catalog No. A554
ISBN 0-7649-1027-2

Interior design by Shannon Lemme

Printed in USA

08 07 06 05 04 03 02 01 00 99   10 9 8 7 6 5 4 3 2 1

Contents

FOREWORD vi
INTRODUCTION vii
RANGER'S WELCOME viii

I. GETTING THERE 1
    Where is Muir Woods? 2
    How do we get there? 4
    What's the best time of year to see Muir Woods? 6
    How much does it cost to get in? 7
    Is Muir Woods always open to visitors? ... 8
    What services are available? 9
    Who runs Muir Woods? 11
    Where can we stay or camp overnight near Muir Woods? ... 12
    Can Fido come, too? 14
    What should we bring? 16

II. ATTRACTIONS 17
    What's there to see and do in Muir Woods? 18
    What's the best way to get oriented? 20
    How long does it take to see Muir Woods? 21
    How old is Muir Woods? 22
    How did visitors get to Muir Woods before automobiles? ... 24
    Why is it called Muir Woods? 26
    What kinds of trees will we see? 28
    Why are the redwood trees so big? 30
    Why do some of the trees have name plaques? 32
    Why is it so quiet in the woods? 33
    What's so interesting about the redwood trees? 34
    Can we drink water from the creek? 36
    What should we look for in Redwood Creek? 38
    What kinds of animals live in Muir Woods? 40
    What's the best way to see wildlife? 42
    Can we feed the animals? 44
    What animals are the most dangerous? 45
    Are there any great birding spots? 46
    Enough about animals! What kinds of plants will we see? ... 49
    Where are the best places to see wildflowers? 51
    Can we see fall color in the woods? 53
    Are there any plants, trees, or areas we should avoid? 54
    Can we see the Pacific Ocean from the woods? 55

How can we avoid crowds? 56
How can we take great pictures of the woods? 57
What can we take home as a memento of our visit? 58

III. RECREATIONAL OPPORTUNITIES .59
What's there to do around here? 60
How much of Muir Woods is accessible to hikers? 62
What do we need to know about hiking
  in and around Muir Woods? 63
Can we take a ranger-led walk? 65
What should we take on our day hike? 67
We'd like a nice, easy day hike. Any suggestions? 68
How about some more challenging hikes? 69
What are some great butt-kicking hikes? 70
Can we mountain bike in Muir Woods? 71
Can we go horseback riding? 72
Are there any good fishing spots? 73
Where can we camp in the area? 74
What are the best beaches in the area? 78

IV. LODGING AND DINING 81
Where can we stay or camp near Muir Woods? 82
Where can we eat in Muir Woods? 85
Where can we dine in the nearby towns? 86
Where are the best picnic spots? 89
Can we hike to any restaurants and inns in the area? 91
Are there any special seasonal events in Muir Woods? 93

THE FUTURE OF MUIR WOODS 95

RANGER'S FAREWELL 96

QUICK REFERENCE 97
Camping and Backpacking Checklist 98
Chronology of Muir Woods National Monument 99
Education Programs: Muir Woods as a Classroom 104
Membership Applications 106
Place Names of Muir Woods and Vicinity 108
Preservation and Conservation Projects in Muir Woods 113
Telephone Directory 114
Telephone Numbers for Greater Muir Woods Area Resources 118

Transportation and Tour Companies Registered to Serve
  Muir Woods 120
Trivia about Muir Woods 122
Volunteer Programs in Muir Woods and Vicinity 125

FURTHER READING 129

INDEX 131

ACKNOWLEDGMENTS 142

ABOUT THE AUTHORS 143

· Foreword ·

For nearly two decades, I've been fortunate enough to get to know Muir Woods as an insider. There is a special satisfaction in knowing a place intimately while retaining a sense of wonder with every walk into this forest of old-growth redwoods. As new questions and insights arise, my awareness of Muir Woods's complexity deepens, and the challenge of stewardship renews my sense of responsibility.

Drawing vision from such early conservationists as John Muir, William Kent, and Alice Eastwood, we stewards have begun to understand the significance of Muir Woods far beyond its role as an attraction for 1.8 million visitors each year. As an old-growth forest located within a protected watershed close to a major metropolitan area, Muir Woods has become a model of the hopes, dreams, and challenges for national parks across the United States. I relish the opportunity to partake in this evolution of purpose and redefinition of function for Muir Woods.

What fuels me are the varied source of inspiration that await around every corner. Whether I'm retelling the lore of the woods to day camp kids, learning the ropes from an older ranger, counting returning salmon, building a new boardwalk, hearing awe expressed in many different languages, or simply filling my lungs with the fresh forest air, I realize the larger purpose of parks and the roles they play in all our lives.

From my early days here, cartoonist Phil Frank has been offering a humorous view of modern Muir Woods. Little has escaped his gentle, lampooning pen, as we dealt with feral pig threats, tour bus crises, and the daily eccentricities of life in the Woods. Now, I join Susan and Phil Frank in inviting you '"inside" Muir Woods. In John Muir's words, welcome to "the best tree-lover's monument that could possibly be found in all the forests of the world"!

Mia Monroe
Muir Woods
April 1999

Introduction

Muir Woods National Monument and the surrounding national and state parklands offer an amazing array of natural wonders, activities, accommodations, and facilities. You'll probably want to ask a few questions to figure out what to do when and how. This book offers you a quick and easy way of finding the answers you need. Your guide through this handbook will be Ranger Mia, who closely resembles Mia Monroe, a veteran ranger who has been at Muir Woods long enough to have heard all the questions that visitors ask—and to know the answers. We thought she would be a natural to guide you through the woods as only an insider can.

The question-and-answer format we use came from a document created by the National Park Service Division of Interpretation at Muir Woods National Monument to help park rangers and interpretive staff there get oriented quickly.

We've updated many of those questions, provided answers specific to Muir Woods, and added lots of others to help you learn some insider information about these magnificent woods and their surroundings. We hope the book will add to your enjoyment of Muir Woods, whatever your interests and however long your visit.

I
Getting there

Where is Muir Woods?

Deep inside a secluded canyon just 12 miles north of San Francisco and about 3 miles from the Pacific Ocean stands a forest of ancient trees known as Muir Woods. Sheltered from prevailing winds and fed by ample rain and moisture from cool summer fog, this 560-acre national monument has a magnificent forest with some of the last remaining old-growth coast redwood trees in California.

Muir Woods is actually a park within a park within a park. It's surrounded by the 6,300-acre Mount Tamalpais State Park and within the boundaries of the 74,000-acre Golden Gate National Recreation Area (GGNRA). The GGNRA stretches along 28 miles of coastline in three counties, from the Presidio of San Francisco to the Marin Headlands north of the Golden Gate Bridge and up the coast to the very tip of the Point Reyes National Seashore. Created in 1972, the GGNRA, commonly known as Golden Gate National Parks, is one of the largest and most varied national parks in an urban setting. Other world-famous landmarks of the GGNRA are Alcatraz Island, the Cliff House, and Fort Point National Historic Site. Muir Woods is the only national monument in the GGNRA and just the sixth area to be designated a national monument in the United States.

At Muir Woods, we also have the dubious distinction of welcoming the most visitors through a single park entrance (1.8 million a year) in the country.

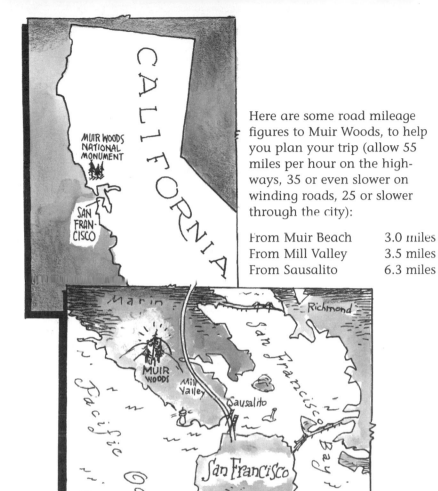

Here are some road mileage figures to Muir Woods, to help you plan your trip (allow 55 miles per hour on the highways, 35 or even slower on winding roads, 25 or slower through the city):

From Muir Beach	3.0 miles
From Mill Valley	3.5 miles
From Sausalito	6.3 miles

From Stinson Beach (via Panoramic Highway)	9.6 miles
From San Francisco (The Presidio)	12 miles
From San Francisco (downtown)	15 miles
From Point Reyes National Seashore Visitor Center	25 miles
From John Muir National Historic Site, Martinez	44 miles
From Napa Valley	53 miles
From Sacramento (state capitol)	91 miles
From Big Sur	165 miles
From Lake Tahoe	200 miles
From Yosemite National Park	208 miles
From Sequoia–Kings Canyon National Park	289 miles
From Redwood National Park	309 miles

You can visit Muir Woods by car, tour vehicle, ferry (plus shuttle), or a combination of public transit and your own power (bicycling or hiking).

By Car. You can drive to Muir Woods if you don't mind steep and winding roads, and your vehicle is less than 35 feet long. The only route available—U.S. Highway 101 to California Highway 1—is quite a roller coaster, winding up and around Mount Tamalpais and then dropping quickly into Muir Woods.

By Commercial Tour. If you want to leave the driving to someone else, take a commercial tour from San Francisco. Choices range from small customized tours of the Marin Headlands and Muir Woods for two to four people in a sports utility vehicle (A Day in Nature: $50 per person) or two to four people in a Jeep Wrangler (Golden Gate Jeep Tours: $35 per person) to larger group tours in microbuses that include both Sausalito and Muir Woods (Gray Line Tours: $33 per person; Tower Tours: $30 per person). For telephone numbers, see the Telephone Directory on page 114; for a list of more tour companies that regularly serve Muir Woods, see page 120 or call your travel agent.

By Ferry. If you want to combine water and land transportation, take a Blue and Gold Ferry from Pier 41 in San Francisco to Tiburon, where a luxury van will take you to the woods for a two-hour self-guided tour and will return you to the ferry for the trip back to San Francisco. This half-day package costs $36 for adults, and $22 for children ages 5–11. Call (415) 705-5444 for schedules and more information.

By Bicycle. If you're game for a strenuous and often treacherous ride, you can tackle Highway 1 on a bicycle. You need to have the skill to negotiate narrow roads with heavy traffic and enough experience to know what it takes to get there and back.

By Hiking. If you want less speed and more scenery, park your car at one of the trailheads in Mount Tamalpais State Park adjacent to Muir Woods and hike down into the woods. Although no public transportation serves the woods, you can take Golden Gate Transit bus 63 (which runs weekends and holidays only) from Marin City to Mountain Home Inn on Panoramic Highway, and then hike down the steep Redwood Trail to Ocean View Trail for 1.8 miles into Muir Woods. For schedule and fee information, call Golden Gate Transit at (415) 923-2000.

The map below shows how to drive to Muir Woods. You'll find more detailed information on getting there by tour (page 120), bicycle (page 71), and hiking (pages 62–70) in other sections of this book.

What's the best time of year to see Muir Woods?

That depends on what you want to see. Forest life never stops; it just makes slight adjustments depending on the season. In all seasons, we suggest that you come to the woods either early or late in the day to avoid our rush hour. You'd be surprised how much more you'll be able to see and hear if you're in the woods during the more dramatic early morning or dusk hours. And don't let wet weather deter you—walking in the rain you'll enjoy the intensified smells and sounds of the forest.

During spring the birds are busy making their nests, wildflowers appear along Redwood Canyon, and our blacktail deer give birth, so you're bound to see does and spotted fawns in the forest. Our summer season is when the big crowds arrive, so it's best to plan your visit on weekdays, early mornings, or late afternoons. Along with the crowds come morning blankets of fog, providing ample moisture for our trees and plants. Summer is when you'll see azaleas bloom throughout the forest, and you'll probably hear the scolding banter of the Steller's jays and see the antics of our chipmunks and ground squirrels. Fall is usually the warmest time of year—the season when ladybugs cluster in horsetail ferns throughout the forest, crayfish crawl along the bottom of Redwood Creek, and the leaves of the big-leaf maples turn golden and fall to the forest floor. In winter, wild and wet storms transform the woods, migratory birds appear, salmon and steelhead swim up Redwood Creek to spawn, and the toyon berries turn a vibrant red.

Because Muir Woods is a forest, with lots of trees to shade the trails, the weather is usually cool and moist year-round. Daytime temperatures average 40 to 70 degrees Fahrenheit. So, no matter which season, bring enough clothing to add and remove layers easily.

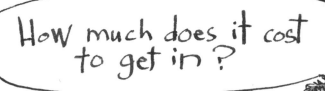

How much does it cost to get in?

A s you walk to the entrance of the main trail you'll pay an entrance fee at the ranger station and receive a brochure with basic park information and a walking map. Commercial tours need to call (415) 388-7368 to make advance reservations. For fee waivers for educational groups, call (415) 388-2596.

Visitors ages 17 and older $2

Children 16 and under . . . . Free

Annual Muir Woods Pass *(good for one year)* $15

Golden Eagle Pass $50

(good for all national parks, monuments, and sites for one year)

Golden Age Pass $10

(lifetime pass to all national parks, monuments, and sites for U.S. citizens who are 62 and older)

Golden Access Pass . . . Free

(for blind or permanently disabled U.S. citizens or permanent residents)

ENTRANCE FEES	
Adults	$2.00
Children (16 yrs. and under)	Free
Golden Eagle Annual Pass	$50.00
Muir Woods Annual Pass	$15.00

Why do Golden Eagles have to pay to get in, Daddy?

Is Muir Woods always open to visitors?

We are open every day of the year from 8 a.m. to sunset to give visitors plenty of time to enjoy a walk in the woods. Since we don't have overnight facilities in the park, our parking lots close at sunset year-round (8 p.m. in the summer).

Although it hasn't happened since 1845, Mother Nature could close Muir Woods with a forest fire. If we have a particularly wet winter, Redwood Creek can flood the trails, and then we have to close certain areas to visitors. However, it's more likely to be the human herding instinct that makes the woods inaccessible. If you come on a weekend afternoon during our summer months, parking can be a problem. We have two parking lots accommodating about 220 vehicles plus a tour bus parking area. When both lots are full, the woods reach maximum visitor capacity, a condition that happens often in our peak season. To avoid the possibility of not getting in, consider coming between November and May, on a weekday, or in the early morning or late afternoon during the summer.

What services are available?

Within Muir Woods's Redwood Canyon, you'll find a visitor center and bookstore, a self-guiding nature trail, exhibits, a café serving breakfast and lunch, a gift shop, telephones, and restrooms. Six miles of mostly level, paved trails and loop walks link to 60 miles of unpaved trails in Mount Tamalpais State Park and out to the Pacific Ocean. Rangers and park service volunteers lead scheduled walks and talks about the history, ecology, and geology of the woods year-round.

If you're looking for grocery stores, delicatessens, or gas stations, you'll have to drive to Mill Valley, 3.5 miles away, or Sausalito, 6 miles away. Although no lodging, camping, or RV facilities are available in Muir Woods, there are hostels, camping areas, and lodgings in the Golden Gate National Recreation Area with easy access to Muir Woods. For more detailed information and telephone numbers, see page 12. Although you won't find any picnic areas in Muir Woods, you will find plenty of wonderful spots to picnic at nearby Muir Beach, Muir Beach Overlook, the Marin Headlands, Mount Tamalpais State Park, and Point Reyes National Seashore. Some of the Bay Area's best restaurants are located in the nearby towns of Mill Valley and Sausalito. For suggestions, see pages 86–88.

Who runs Muir Woods?

The United States National Park Service (NPS), which is part of the Department of the Interior, protects resources and people in Muir Woods National Monument. This means you won't see any highway patrol officers, sheriffs, or municipal firefighters during your visit.

But plenty of NPS people are around to make sure things run smoothly. Park rangers handle law enforcement, traffic regulation, search and rescue, and other duties. Park naturalists and volunteer interpreters provide all the educational walks, talks, and programs in Muir Woods. The people dressed in green pants, gray shirts, and the famous Stetson ranger hats are ranger interpreters, and the ones wearing the dark green baseball caps may be rangers, interpreters, or field maintenance, fire, and resource management workers. As site supervisor, I oversee daily operations and report on a regular basis to the managers and the superintendent of the Golden Gate National Recreation Area.

To help with other park services, the NPS has a contract with a private concession company, Aramark, which runs our café and gift shop, charging prices authorized by the NPS. The visitor center is managed by the Golden Gate National Parks Association (GGNPA), a nonprofit organization that supports NPS programs by collecting park fees, managing the bookstore, publishing visitor information, funding wildlife conservation projects, spearheading new visitor services and events, and organizing active volunteer efforts. GGNPA staff members wear black pants and green shirts.

You can contact the NPS, Aramark, or the GGNPA at the following numbers:

National Park Service
Muir Woods National Monument
Mill Valley, CA 94941-2696
(415) 388-2595
www.nps.gov/muwo

Golden Gate National
Parks Association
Fort Mason, Building 201
San Francisco, CA 94123
(415) 388-7368

Aramark Corporation
Muir Woods
National
Monument
Mill Valley, CA
94941-2696
(415) 388-7059

GOLDEN GATE
NATIONAL
PARKS
ASSOCIATION

★ ARAMARK

A lthough there are no lodging or camping places inside the boundary of Muir Woods, there are some great choices nearby. Since the numbers of rooms and campsites are more limited the closer you get to the woods, it's best to reserve well before your arrival.

The closest lodgings are the Mountain Home Inn, with just ten rooms, about 3.5 miles from the entrance to Muir Woods via the upper road, and the Pelican Inn, with seven rooms, located 2.5 miles from the lower road entrance to the woods. Because of their unique and spectacular locations, prices are a little steep (and subject to change): from $139 to $259 at the Mountain Home Inn, (415) 381-9000, and $184 to $209 at the Pelican Inn, (415) 383-6000. All rates include full breakfast and access to some of the most beautiful trails and vistas in the GGNRA. Other nearby lodgings are conveniently located in Mill Valley and Sausalito. For a list of selected hotels, motels, and bed-and-breakfast inns, check pages 82–84.

The closest camping, within 3 miles of Muir Woods, is in the adjacent Mount Tamalpais State Park, which offers two campgrounds, each having a small number of sites. One is located at the Pan Toll Ranger Station at the summit of Mount Tamalpais (elevation 1,200 feet). Here you'll find sixteen sites with tables, fire pits with grills, and bathrooms (no showers). These are available only on a first-come, first-served basis and cost $16 a night (weekends), $15 (weekdays), from April to October, and $12 the rest of the year. Call (415) 388-2070 for more information. The second campground is at Steep Ravine near Stinson Beach. Six primitive campsites and ten rustic cabins are perched on a steep hill overlooking the Pacific Ocean. Outhouses serve as toilets, and the closest shower is the ocean. Cabins go for $30 year-round, and campsites cost $11 from April to

October, $7 the rest of the year. To reserve space at Steep Ravine, call (800) 444-7275.

If you have a group of ten or more, the two group campsites at Alice Eastwood Group Camp in Mount Tamalpais State Park near Muir Woods cost $37.50 per night for groups from ten to twenty-five people, and $75 for twenty-five to fifty people. Permits are required. To reserve a site, call (800) 444-7275. Other campgrounds are located throughout the GGNRA, including several at the Point Reyes National Seashore. For more camping information, see pages 74–77.

Can Fido come, too?

The main self-guiding trail along Redwood Canyon in Muir Woods is a narrow path where 1.8 million visitors a year slowly meander through the quiet forest setting of the woods. It's not exactly the perfect place to play fetch with Fido.

For that reason, dogs have been prohibited in Muir Woods since 1974. But it's not just canines that are restricted. Due to the rapidly growing number of visitors, we can't accommodate camping or picnicking in the woods. More recently, we had to build fences to keep visitors on the paved trails—and off the plants.

These rules were made for good reason. Our fragile forest ecosystem isn't ready for the wild mountain chihuahua or free-range labrador. With so many people in such a small area, it's hard enough to keep visitors from inadvertently trampling plants and keep well-meaning children from unknowingly breaking young redwood sprouts. Add canines to the mix, and you can imagine the potential problems for park wildlife and their natural habitats, not to mention other visitors. Park rangers keep careful watch about these regulations, and they're not shy about handing out citations to those who break the rules.

Dogs left unattended inside cars while their owners walk in the woods create another problem. Because of the possible safety hazard to the animals, not to mention the noise created when a chorus of barking drifts into the woods from the parking lots, we recommend that you leave your canine friends at home during your visit to Muir Woods.

You can, however, walk your pooch on trails in some beautiful areas surrounding Muir Woods. Refer to page 15 for a map of dog-friendly trails.

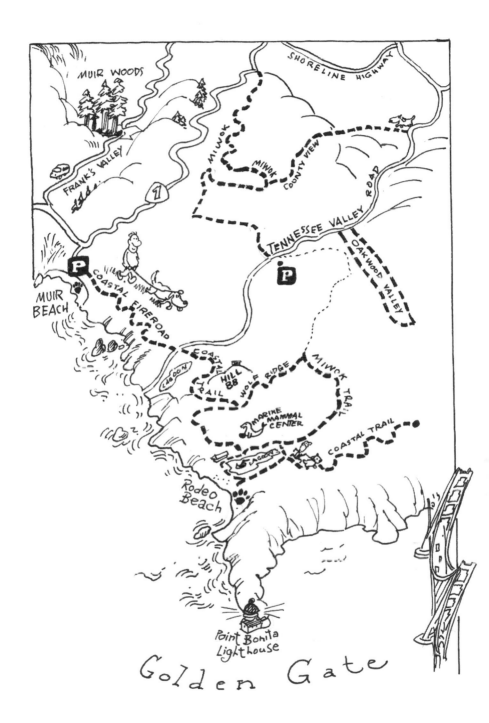

W hat you bring to Muir Woods depends on your accommodations and activities of choice, but I can tell you some basic items that will make your trip more comfortable. For advice on special activities, turn to the Recreational Opportunities section of this book.

Our weather is generally predictable. In fact, the weather hasn't changed here since the time dinosaurs roamed the area. The park is cool, shaded, and moist all year, with daytime temperatures averaging 40 to 70 degrees Fahrenheit. We get up to 50 inches of rain, primarily during the winter months, and a fair amount of moist fog during the summer. To be comfortable, dress in layers, so you can add and subtract as needed. Don't forget a raincoat or parka with a hood and sturdy hiking boots or walking shoes. A pair of gloves and a cap for your head are also advisable. If you plan to hike out of the redwood groves, it's best to wear long sleeves and pants to protect yourself from ticks.

There are drinking fountains on the main canyon path, but you need to carry water if you hike out of the canyon, and don't forget a map to keep you on the right trail. A notebook for writing and a sketch pad are always good companions in the woods. Binoculars will help you spot our birds and other animals, and a camera will record proof that you were here.

SEASONAL WEATHER

	Jan	Feb	Mar	Apr	May	June	July	Aug	Sept	Oct	Nov	Dec
Precipitation*	8.16	5.94	5.09	2.32	0.96	0.40	0.09	0.18	0.48	2.07	5.33	6.61
High (°F)**	57.5	58.7	62.0	63.0	63.2	68.2	69.4	73.2	72.7	74.3	61.7	58.8
Low (°F)**	45.0	44.6	43.5	46.9	46.3	51.0	50.8	51.3	52.1	46.2	42.9	37.5

*Precipitation based on fifty-year average (inches)
**1998 average temperatures

III
Attractions

What's there to see and do in Muir Woods?

If you're looking for great hiking with sweeping views of San Francisco and the Pacific Ocean, welcome to paradise. Muir Woods is also one of the few places in the world where you can still stroll among a grove of old-growth coast redwoods in one of California's last surviving virgin redwood forests. To walk in Muir Woods is to walk back in time—to the days when trees outnumbered people and plentiful wildlife roamed the hills and lowland valleys surrounding San Francisco Bay.

Muir Woods's 560 acres include 6 miles of walking trails that connect with 60 miles of trails throughout Mount Tamalpais State Park. The trails range from an easy 1-mile paved Main Loop Trail along the floor of Redwood Canyon to hikes up to the top of Mount Tamalpais, where you can enjoy a picnic while gazing at a spectacular view of the Pacific Ocean and San Francisco.

A walk in the woods here also gives you unique up-close views of the plant and animal life of a redwood forest. Not only can you see some of the oldest and the tallest trees in the world, but you can also discover aquatic life in the seasonal rushing rapids and quiet pools of Redwood Creek. Depending upon the time of year, you'll see and learn about the life cycles of monarch butterflies, salmon, mushrooms, wildflowers, ladybugs, blacktail deer, birds, chipmunks, and other forest residents.

If you have only a short time to spend, take the Hillside Trail, which leads you above Redwood Canyon for a magnificent view into the woods below. Taking the chance to sit, write, or sketch quietly on one of the benches located throughout the woods, you can absorb sounds, smells, and views of forest life that you otherwise might miss. One of my favorite things to do is to walk through the woods with a kid—the forest comes to life when you see it through the eyes of a child.

If you have a little more time to spend, I suggest the 3-hour round-trip hike starting in Muir Woods, up Ben Johnson Trail, along the scenic Dipsea Trail, and back to the woods. The route provides breathtaking ocean and city views as well as opportunities to experience many of the plant communities found throughout the Golden Gate National Recreation Area.

For those who like reading about nature, the visitor center offers exhibits and an excellent selection of books about Muir Woods and redwood forests. There's even a cozy fireside reading or writing area. Or join a ranger or park service volunteer on one of the regularly scheduled interpretive walks and talks in the woods. Call (415) 388-2595 for times and locations.

Make your first stop at the information table in front of the visitor center if it's open for business—every day during the summer months and limited times in the winter. The table is staffed by knowledgeable park service volunteers who can give you good advice about the woods or sell you a trail map to guide you on your way.

The visitor center is always a good place to begin your excursion to Muir Woods. Within its 700 square feet you'll find exhibits, an informed staff, and a bookstore filled with educational books, games, and merchandise that will give you a better understanding of what you see in the woods. The children's area has some great selections for kids who want to become "nature detectives." One of my favorites is the bug box, which helps you catch, magnify, and release bugs without harming them. For $1, you can pick up a park brochure in German, Spanish, French, and Japanese. And sitting in front of the fireplace to read about Muir Woods is always a pleasant way to begin or end your trek through the woods.

As you venture out on your own, you might want to hook up with one of our fifteen-minute interpretive talks or walks—a great way to get the inside scoop about the woods. Our rangers offer these talks and walks year-round at various locations through Redwood Canyon. Check at the information table or visitor center for times and locations, or call (415) 388-2595 for details.

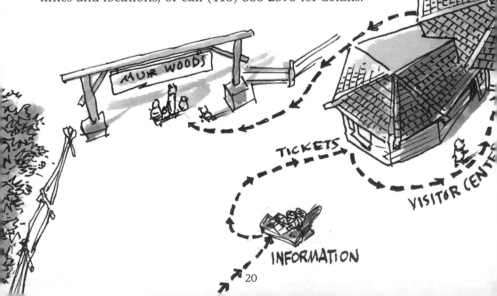

> **How long does it take to see Muir Woods?**

That depends on how much of the woods you want to see. We usually say it takes about two hours, in which time you can walk the Main Loop Trail from the visitor center to the fourth footbridge, and return via the Hillside Trail (2 miles). That still leaves you time to stop at the café, gift shop, bookstore, and visitor center. On your next visit you'll be a seasoned veteran, ready to learn more about the woods on a ranger-led walk and tackle some of the other trails.

If you have less time, try the 1-mile Main Loop Trail from the visitor center to Cathedral Grove and back. Then stop for a quick lunch or snack at the café, or visit the gift shop. You can finish your whirlwind tour by checking out the visitor center and bookstore, and you'll still leave the woods within an hour and a half of your arrival.

If you have more time, we always recommend a longer tour of the woods, which might include one of the trails up out of the canyon. A complete Muir Woods experience includes some quiet time in the woods, a lingering lunch in the café, and a chance to browse the visitor center for books about the area.

Whatever amount of time you can spend seeing the woods, whether it's your first or hundredth time, will be time you'll savor in one of California's most beautiful and serene settings.

How old is Muir Woods?

The big story starts 20 million to 30 million years ago. That's when trees resembling the coast redwood grew in scattered places across the Northern Hemisphere. After surviving climate changes, geologic upheavals, and the Ice Age, the coast redwood exists today only along a narrow strip of land 475 miles long, reaching from southwestern Oregon to the Big Sur coast in California. The trees are almost always found near the ocean where rain and coastal fog are plentiful.

Some geologists think rainstorms and an earthquake caused a huge landslide around Mount Tamalpais tens of thousands of years ago. This prehistoric slide sent soil and boulders down the west wall of the mountain to the land around its base (present-day Mill Valley and Muir Woods). Over a period of thousands of years, creeks carved deep canyons like the one where Muir Woods stands today. Sheltered from winds and fed by year-round rain and fog, the redwoods grew and prospered in this canyon, creating a unique ecosystem filled with plants and animals attracted by the moist, low-light conditions. The trees reached majestic heights and eventually acquired life cycles that often exceeded 600 years. Over the centuries, their growth was slowed by occasional fires, floods, or droughts.

The Coast Miwok people established villages near the shoreline of San Francisco Bay about 2,000 years ago. Although they found their primary foods in the water, the Miwok probably also hunted small game in the area's rolling hills and canyon forests such as Muir Woods. The arrival of Spanish traders and adventurers in the 1700s brought the decline of the Coast Miwok and use of the surrounding wildlands for private purposes, including grazing and tree cutting.

Happy Birthday to you... ♪

In 1838, Muir Woods was included in a Spanish land grant, Rancho Sausalito, issued to an English settler, William Richardson. At about the same time, people began logging redwoods in areas close to water transportation to build the new city of San Francisco (then called Yerba Buena). Because of its isolated location, Muir Woods was saved from the fate of most of the area's redwood forests.

In the late 1880s, first horseback riders and then passengers of the Mount Tamalpais and Muir Woods Railway began to make the trek from nearby Mill Valley to what was then known as Redwood or Sequoia Canyon. Word of the great trees spread. By the turn of the century, more efficient logging and transportation methods made the woods more vulnerable to cutting. The owners of the canyon, feeling pressure to sell the valuable timberland, approached William Kent, a local resident and early conservationist.

Kent purchased the woods for $45,000 just one year before the San Francisco earthquake and fire of 1906, an event that probably would have led to wholesale logging of the woods as part of the massive effort to rebuild the devastated city. The final threat came in 1907, when a local water company sued to condemn most of the canyon for a reservoir that would supply the burgeoning communities around Mount Tamalpais. Kent launched a campaign to save the woods by donating them to the federal government. With the help of Gifford Pinchot, then U.S. Chief Forester, Kent convinced President Theodore Roosevelt to preserve Redwood Canyon for the nation, and on January 9, 1908, the president proclaimed Kent's gift a national monument.

So, although the name Muir Woods National Monument dates from only 1908, the woods, including their old-growth coast redwoods and virgin forest, have been in the same location for at least a thousand years.

A California Redwood Tree

How did visitors get to Muir Woods before automobiles?

A few rode in on horses, but the majority came by rail. Between 1896 and 1930, visitors could ride to the top of Mount Tamalpais aboard the Mount Tamalpais and Muir Woods Railway, following a switchback track known as "The Crookedest Railroad in the World."

Early visitors would arrive in Mill Valley by ferry and train, then switch over to the open observation cars of the Mount Tamalpais Railway. With the engine pushing, the cars filled with people would climb up the mountainside, providing riders with an ever-changing panorama all the way. At the summit were a tavern and hotel where visitors could enjoy lunch on a glassed-in veranda with spectacular views of the city 13 miles away.

Eventually, the conductor would call out "All aboard for the gravity ride to Muir Woods." The more adventuresome visitors climbed aboard the little gravity cars in groups of fifteen. When the seats were filled, the brakeman took his place, released the hand brake, and let the cars begin their descent.

At a point in the descent known as Double Bow Knot, the cars entered the woods. The brakeman rang a bell to alert deer or occasional hikers who might be crossing the tracks. As the cars went deeper into the forest, they rounded a bend and coasted to a stop in front of the Muir Woods Inn.

Each day, other trains, with steam engines and covered cars, would arrive with the more fainthearted travelers. Visitors were free to explore Muir Woods and wander among the giant redwoods before climbing back on the train for the return trip. The little gravity cars

The Double Bow Knot on the Mt. Tamalpais Railway, overlooking San Francisco Bay and City.

were hooked to the front of the steam engine, with the closed cars attached to the rear. The train would push and pull its load back up the mountain and then descend into Mill Valley.

Was it a great ride? In thirty-four years of operation, no one ever asked for a refund. You can still travel the railroad route when you hike up or down Gravity Car Grade.

Why is it called Muir Woods?

When William Kent donated the first 300 acres to the federal government to be preserved as a national monument for future generations to enjoy, he never intended the woods to become a monument to himself. So he requested that it be named in honor of environmentalist John Muir.

John Muir

Although the name Muir Woods had a nice ring to it, President Theodore Roosevelt instead suggested that the woods be named Kent Monument, to honor its public-spirited benefactor. To this, Kent responded, "Your kind suggestion of a change of name is not one that I can accept. . . . I have five good husky boys that I am trying to bring up to a knowledge of democracy and to a realizing sense of the rights of the 'other fellow,' doctrines which you, sir, have taught with more vigor and effect than any other man in my time. If these boys cannot keep the name Kent alive, I am willing it should be forgotten."

For his part, John Muir spent his life traveling and studying nature and humanity's relation to it. He wrote prolifically about the fragility and importance of America's untouched natural areas, including Yosemite before it became a national park. Muir is generally thought of as America's first conservationist—a major figure in winning public acceptance of conservation as an environmental ethic—inspiring generations of wilderness advocates.

Deferring to Kent's wishes, Roosevelt declared Muir Woods a national monument in 1908. William Kent originally saved the woods because they were the only redwood forest left uncut in the Bay Area. A century later, Muir Woods is now one of only two protected old-growth redwood forests in the world—a fitting tribute to John Muir.

John Muir, William Kent, and unidentified man in front of Inn

IN JOHN MUIR'S WORDS

"If people in general could be got into the woods, even for once, to hear the trees speak for themselves, all difficulties in the way of forest preservation would vanish."

"The clearest way into the Universe is through a forest wilderness."

"I went out for a walk and finally concluded to stay out until sundown for going out I found I was really going in."

"Everybody needs beauty as well as bread, places to play in and pray in, where Nature may heal and cheer and give strength to body and soul alike."

"[The redwoods are] the first to touch the rosy beams of morning, the last to bid the sun goodnite."

"[Muir Woods] is the best tree-lover's monument that could possibly be found in all the forests of the world."

"It is good to know that mountain and forest [Muir Woods and Mount Tamalpais] will be there, open and unspoiled for them [children], so they may know of nature to the health of their souls."

What kind of trees will we see?

Although the tall, majestic coast redwoods dominate Muir Woods, they're not the only trees you'll see. Let's take a walk through the different areas of the forest to see how many other types of trees we can identify.

Mingled among the redwoods on the forest floor you'll see an abundance of bigleaf maples and bay trees (laurels). The leaves of the maples turn a brilliant orange and gold in the fall, and the leaves of the bays have a spicy aroma when rubbed between your fingers. Along the lower end of Redwood Creek you'll find red alders. Members of the birch family, they are easily recognized by their patchy gray-white bark, coarsely toothed leaves, and clusters of long catkins in the spring. Occasionally mixed in with the redwoods, you'll see a tanbark oak with its shiny, thick, oval leaves. Its acorns are the favorite food of our squirrels and deer.

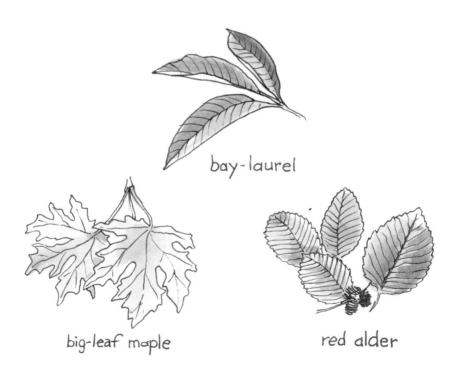

bay-laurel

big-leaf maple

red alder

At the edge of the redwood forest grow Douglas fir and California buckeye trees. You'll recognize the buckeye by its compound leaves and clusters of white or reddish flowers. The Douglas fir is the woods' other tall tree, and it's more susceptible to death from fires and floods than its taller neighbor. But it's no wimp, either. Douglas fir can grow in less hospitable conditions than redwood, and the spread of these trees into a forest or grassland is our first clue that the area may no longer support the demands of water-hungry redwoods.

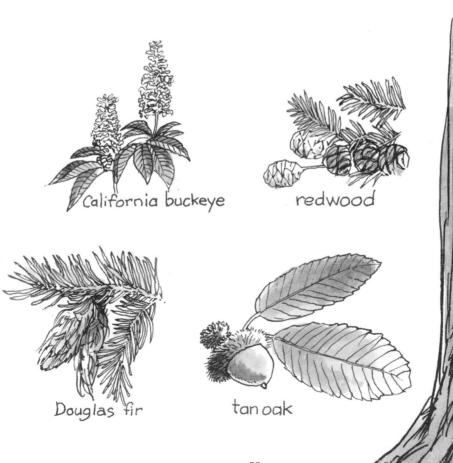

California buckeye

redwood

Douglas fir

tan oak

Why are the redwood trees so big?

L ongevity and location, location, location. The coast redwoods found in Muir Woods are examples of the tallest trees in the world—one is 252 feet tall, another is 14 feet wide, and some are at least 1,000 years old. Why? Part of the answer has to do with human factors and climate, part with the natural physiology of these amazing trees.

While most old-growth coast redwood trees were cut for timber, the redwoods in Muir Woods and other California and Oregon national and state parks were protected from logging through the efforts of early conservationists. Once protected, these trees had the chance to grow for a full life cycle—which can be as long as 2,000 years. If you consider that a young coast redwood can grow as much as 12 inches a year, that's a lot of tree.

Climatic features complete the formula for big redwoods: our coastal fog belt provides just the right amount of year-round moisture for the coast redwood to flourish, and our deep canyons protect the trees from wind and salt spray. The root system of a redwood is specially designed to take in lots of water.

The roots normally go down only 6–8 feet, but they spread way out (50 feet or more) just below the surface, gathering moisture from fog-drip as well as rain. The only flaw in this design is that the shallow roots don't provide a very stable base for the huge trees. For that reason, redwoods are susceptible to being toppled by occasional strong winds.

The fact that redwoods apparently do not suffer the physiological effects of aging also plays a part in their large size. Few trees are as well equipped to defend against natural enemies. As a matter of fact, there are no known killing diseases for an established redwood and no built-in reason for any particular redwood tree to die at all (barring accidents involving wind and fire). Redwoods change as they age, and their growth slows. But, remarkably, deterioration is not inevitable.

When you're deep in the woods, it's awesome to look up and imagine the length of time and scope of human events that are encompassed by the life of one big tree.

In the early days, it used to be standard practice to name redwood trees for important people, causes, and events. The name was usually placed on the tree with a commemorative plaque. Muir Woods has six named trees: Ralph Waldo Emerson (1903); Gifford Pinchot (1910); Andrew Jay Cross (1926); William Kent (1928); Franklin Delano Roosevelt and the United Nations (1945); and the most recent addition, the Bicentennial tree (1976).

All of the dedicated trees are found in Redwood Canyon except the Kent tree, a Douglas fir located along Fern Creek Trail as you walk up out of the woods. The story goes that the 273-foot tree used to be the tallest in Muir Woods. That was before its top broke off, making it a mere 224 feet. Of all the trees in the woods, this one was William Kent's favorite.

The choice of a particular tree for a commemorative plaque was most often random, although a few were made for specific reasons, like the Kent tree. Usually the dedication ceremony giving a tree its plaque was quite an event, attended by family, friends, and civic leaders. Gradually, the park service had to prohibit the labeling of trees in the woods, for ecological reasons. An exception was made in 1976 for the Bicentennial tree, chosen because it shared the same 200-year birthday as the United States.

As you walk through the woods, see if you can find these six elusive tree plaques and their fading inscriptions. You can read more about the people who are honored with plaques from the books in Further Reading, on page 129.

Why is it so quiet in the woods?

Muir Woods is world famous for its peace and quiet. Our trees aren't loud, and neither is our animal life, which is limited because the shaded conditions in a redwood forest provide scarce food. Many of the animals, such as our owls and bats, feed at night. Others, such as our deer, roam in the early morning and around dusk. In the day, when most visitors walk our trails, it's really quiet.

The silent voices of most forest residents are a perfect fit with the tranquillity of the woods. If you think about how much noise a squirrel, deer, banana slug, salmon, bat, or mountain lion makes, you'll begin to understand why you won't hear many sounds here. It's so quiet in the woods that often the only sounds you'll hear are those of visitors and an occasional Steller's jay or raven. We like the stillness so much that we have an annual "quiet period" in the woods between February 15 and July 15, during which we don't allow anything noisier than conversation. This helps support the woods' quiet ambiance and protects the habitats of our more reclusive residents, such as the spotted owl. To create this environment, we restrict park trucks to electric vehicles and bar large tour groups from going beyond the café and gift shop. We even work with commercial airlines to keep jets from flying over the woods.

Many people come specifically to enjoy the peace, to think, write, sketch, or walk the forest trails. We encourage visitors to experience the tranquillity of the woods and to see themselves as stewards of this magical place called Muir Woods.

The coast redwood, or *Sequoia sempervirens* (evergreen sequoia), is an amazing tree. Not only is it the tallest species of tree on Earth, but it also has an enormous life span, a unique method of reproduction, and a resistance to decay that makes it among the strongest species in the plant kingdom. Let's take a look at the redwoods in Muir Woods, and I'll show you some of their secrets.

First, not all the redwoods here are exactly alike. Genetic variations produce different foliage colors ranging from light to dark green, different bark textures, and branch structures that give the trees differing shapes. If you walk on the Main Loop Trail near the Pinchot tree you'll see a curly-bark redwood, one of only three known to be living in Muir Woods.

Unlike other cone-bearing trees, the coast redwood reproduces from both seed and sprout. You'll probably see sprouts growing out of normally dormant buds (or burls) at the bases of tree trunks as you walk along the self-guiding trail. Fallen trees and logs can also sprout, although these shoots won't grow into trees unless they can tap into a root system. Even sprouts can vary in color. See if you can spot one of the rare albino (white) redwood sprouts that grow in only three places in the woods. You can also look for a family circle—an ancient parent tree or snag surrounded by younger trees grown from sprouts.

Depending upon the time of year, you may find cones with seeds inside on the forest floor. Pollination of the redwood's reproductive organs, called *strobili*, occurs in January and February. Cones mature to open and release seeds in fall or early winter. Although thousands of seeds drift down to the forest floor, only about 1 percent will germinate, and even fewer will become trees

The redwood is famous for its resistance to insects, rot, and fire. We think tannic acid in the thick bark helps repel insects and mold, and the absence of resin makes the wood difficult to ignite. The trick to guessing the age of redwoods is explained in a 6-foot cross-section of a trunk near the entrance to the woods. You'll see annual rings for the entire life span of the tree, from A.D. 909 to 1930. From this example, see if you can guess the age of other trees.

First, you have to understand the importance of Redwood Creek to the life of the woods. This free-flowing stream that runs through Muir Woods originates at an elevation of 2,000 feet on the southern slopes of Mount Tamalpais. When it leaves the woods, it travels to Muir Beach, where it empties into the Pacific Ocean. Although the watershed of the creek is small—about 8 square miles—it is critical to the survival of a rich diversity of life, specific habitats, and its own distinct microclimate. The National Park Service recognizes the Redwood Creek watershed as a unique ecological area (see the watershed map on page 37).

When you think about taking water from the creek, consider the consequences to the aquatic life it supports. Redwood Creek is home to endangered and diminishing species such as the coho salmon, steelhead trout, and western pond turtle. Along the creek bottom you'll find schools of native critters with names such as three-spined stickleback and riffle sculpin. The stream's riffles, pools, cascades, and flatwater are fragile habitats for a world of aquatic life that is easily disturbed, especially by humans.

The year-round water quality of the creek helps determine the survival and successful return of spawning salmon and steelhead trout each year. Even dipping your hands into the creek can interfere with the delicate and critical balance of natural ingredients needed for spawning habitats. You also risk getting giardiasis, an intestinal ailment caused by an organism in untreated water. Instead of drinking water from the creek, use our water fountains, and observe creek life from the trails and footbridges.

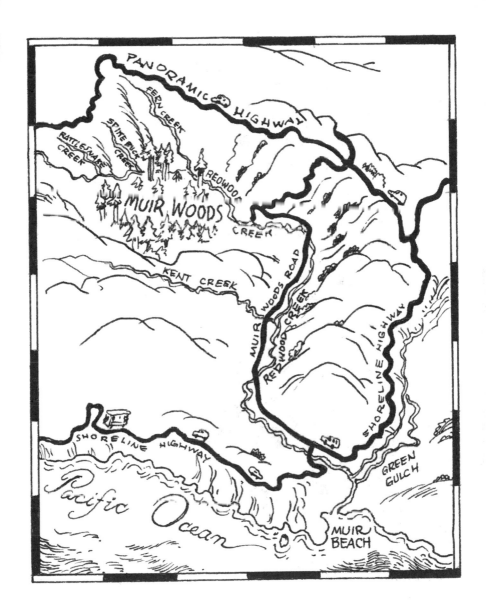

What should we look for in Redwood Creek?

A walk along the creek will let you discover its unique delights. The first sound you'll probably hear is a riffle, a fast-flowing, turbulent area in the creek. Riffles bring oxygen into the water, clean silt and other particles from the creek, provide insects for hungry fish, and create spawning grounds for adult salmon.

Pools are great observation areas. Their deep, slow-moving water is favored by young salmon and crayfish as they forage on insects. Usually a big pool has one big trout, too. The pool above the second bridge, known as Dan Sealy's Pool, usually has a sizable rainbow trout circling in it. A large backwater pool in lower Redwood Creek near Muir Beach can be accessed by a footbridge. If you're there on a sunny day, you might even get to see a pond turtle basking on a log.

Once a rare sight on the creek, cascades are now more common, as fallen trees and forest debris create natural barriers to the flowing water. You'll notice two cascades on the walk from Muir Woods to Muir Beach. A good example of a human-made cascade can be found where the creek runs next to the Muir Woods parking lot just below the bus parking area. The water drops 5 feet over boulders that were added in the 1930s as part of an effort to build a wall along the left bank of the creek.

Flat water is a gliding stretch of water with a slower, deeper, steadier flow than a riffle. A common site in Redwood Creek, flat waters are often sandwiched between riffles and pools. Flat water areas with good cover, such as big boulders or overhanging plants, provide excellent fish and crayfish habitats. The crayfish you'll see are a non-native species with colorful blue and red claws.

Lots of aquatic insects live in Redwood Creek, including stone flies, mayflies, caddis flies, dragonflies, and damselflies. Their life cycles start in the water and then move into the air, where they fly, mate, and die. Once their time in the water is over, generally in the summer months, they shed their shells and wait for their bodies and soft wings to dry and harden. You may see the dried insect shells, or skeletons, on a log or rock. Before they die, female aquatic insects return to the water to lay their eggs.

Other examples of life in the creek include great blue herons and kingfishers (who come to feast on baby fish) and water striders (who can be seen darting along the water's surface).

The seasons change the activity of Redwood Creek. During the dry summers, the water level sinks, and the creek slows. In drought years, the flow may stop in some areas of the creek but the pools continue to sustain life. Winter rains make the water level rise, carving new banks and beds, which last until the next wet season changes the contours again. The creek roars through Muir Woods during our rainy months, pulling silt off the banks and turning the water murky. This is the spawning season, when adult salmon and steelhead make an arduous journey from the Pacific Ocean up to the tiny pockets of Redwood Creek to lay their eggs. Spring and early summer are busy times for creek life. Coho salmon and steelhead trout hatch, and insects gather to chew leaves and algae.

A good source of more information about life in Redwood Creek is *Web of Water: Life in Redwood Creek*, by Maya Khosla, available at the visitor center.

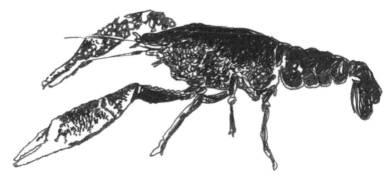

What kinds of animals live in the woods?

An old-growth forest such as Muir Woods provides animals with food as well as cover. The huge trees protect animals from harsh weather and offer good hiding places from predators. When you walk in the woods you'll have a chance to see many forest residents—from large mammals to tiny insects.

In spring and summer, black-tailed deer come here to escape larger predators and to feed on lush forest greens. Does and fawns eat our huckleberry, salal, blackberry, and coltsfoot. In the fall, bucks take their harems up the slopes of Mount Tamalpais, where they all forage on lichen and dry grass during the winter. Our more elusive predators, the gray fox and the bobcat, spend their daylight hours on the higher slopes of the woods. These secretive animals use the cover of night to come into the valley to hunt voles, wood rats, and mice. Raccoons move in and out under cover of night, cruising the creeks, looking for crayfish, grubs, worms, salmon, and acorns. Striped skunks come for anything they can find. Although once extinct from the area, the mountain lion and the coyote have been seen in the upper areas of the woods and should both be avoided by people. Bear and elk were once common forest dwellers, but they have been crowded out of the woods by human activity and development.

Fifty species of birds spend either the entire year or a season in Muir Woods. The Steller's jay and the black raven lend their voices to the forest, while the winter wren and Hutton's vireo hunt insects along Redwood Creek. Other feathered residents include Oregon juncos, brown creepers, nuthatches, and bushtits. In summer, a pair of mallard ducks and an occasional great blue heron come to swim and fish in the creek. In fall, flocks of warblers, flycatchers,

40

golden-crowned kinglets, and varied thrushes arrive in the woods. Our night hunters include bats and northern spotted owls. Near the entrance to the woods, outside the redwood groves, live scrub jays, great horned owls, an occasional Cooper's hawk, and, in early summer, coveys of quail.

Many small mammals live in the forest. The western gray squirrel with its all-purpose bushy tail jumps from tree to tree in search of acorns and cones, while the black-striped Sonoma chipmunk stays closer to the forest floor gathering grasses, seeds, and berries. The dusky-footed wood rat builds its nest in large fallen logs in the forest to protect itself from the spotted owl, while the broad-footed mole builds subsurface tunnels that help aerate the soil. Weighing just 1 ounce, the red-backed vole is one of the woods' smallest mammals, and the only fungivorous mammal in North America. It plays an important role by feeding on fungi below the ground and then dispersing spores throughout the forest, helping the trees take in vital nutrients from the forest soil.

Redwood Creek is home to crayfish (year-round), spawning salmon (December–January) and steelhead (February–March), and newly hatched salmon and steelhead fry(early spring). Reptiles include the western garter snake, the rubber boa, and several species of lizard. The wet season hosts banana slugs and a variety of amphibians, including the California newt and lots of salamanders. Beginning in May, ladybugs come to the woods, and in fall they cluster in masses on the horsetail ferns and other plants.

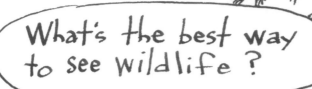

What's the best way to see wildlife?

Looking for animals in a redwood forest can be a challenging task, since many animals use the forest as a hiding place. It requires time, patience, and cunning observation.

The first thing to know about our forest residents is that they feed in the early morning and late afternoon or evening hours. If you can get here by 8 a.m., when we open, or stay until just before we close at sunset, your chances of seeing wildlife increase. These are also the best times to miss the crowds of humans. Large noisy groups of people usually frighten away our quiet forest animals.

You might want to wear dark fabrics, because they blend more naturally with the forest than light ones do. Walk slowly, and, if you see an animal, avoid sudden movements. Don't forget binoculars for "up-close" viewing from a distance. Most importantly, don't try to get too close to the animals. Feeding a squirrel or chipmunk so that you can capture the moment with a photo may seem like a good idea, but these animals have sharp teeth, and if they're sick you could get an infection.

Here are some hints on places to view certain animals. From spring through summer, look for black-tailed deer feeding on the cloverlike oxalis that thrives under redwoods. If you hike in the higher slopes of the woods, you might catch a glimpse of one of our predators— gray foxes, coyotes, bobcats, and the seldom-seen mountain lion. Along Redwood Creek, although you probably won't see any raccoons, you may see their handlike prints in the soft earth.

The bird you'll see most frequently is the Steller's jay, a large, crested, blue-and-black bird whose noisy banter can be heard any time of day in the woods. You might hear the distinctive caw of the black raven high above the forest floor or the hammering of the red-headed pileated woodpecker. Look for the small winter wren, a melodious brown bird that can be seen hunting insects along Redwood Creek. It shares this hunting ground with the Hutton's vireo, a green-gray bird with whitish wing bars and a broken white eye ring.
Feathered residents who can some-

times be seen working up and down tree trunks include brown creepers, nuthatches, and bushtits. Keep your eyes open for a pair of mallard ducks who spend the summer in Redwood Creek and a great blue heron who occasionally comes to fish here. In the early evening, look for bats around hollow redwood snags. Another nocturnal hunter, the northern spotted owl, might be seen anywhere in the woods—perched on branches of the tallest trees, nesting in broken tops, snags, and cavities of lower trees, or flying over the forest floor in search of its favorite food, the dusky-footed wood rat.

Near the entrance to the woods, outside the redwood groves, look for scrub jays, and listen for the sound of great horned owls in the evening. You may also see a Cooper's hawk hunting for prey and, in early summer, quail scurrying by with their platoons of young.

Of our smallest mammals, the western gray squirrel is sometimes seen stripping redwood bark from fallen logs or trunks, in preparation for building a treetop nest, or jumping from tree to tree in search of nuts and cones. Sonoma chipmunks often rest on rocks or stumps as they snack on grasses, seeds, and berries. In large fallen logs in the forest, you might see the nests of dusky-footed wood rats. If you notice any subsurface tunnels, they're probably the work of our broad-footed moles. These tunnels help aerate the soil and allow rain to penetrate, reducing erosion and flooding. Tiny red-backed voles might be spotted running across a bed of moss or up an old tree stump.

Look into Redwood Creek to see crayfish year-round. Salmon spawn there in December and January and steelhead in February and March. The newly hatched salmon and steelhead school in the early spring. During the wet season, look in or near our streams, in damp cavities, or under rotting logs to catch a glimpse of our fragile-skinned amphibians, including newts and salamanders. If you visit the woods in September or October, you're sure to see dazzling clusters of ladybugs on the horsetail ferns that thrive near Redwood Creek and along Bootjack and Fern Creek Trails.

Can we feed the animals?

Sorry, no petting zoo privileges here. Every time someone feeds an animal in Muir Woods, a little bit of the "wild" is stolen from our wildlife. Human food not only may damage the animals' health but also can endanger their survival by luring them away from their natural habits.

Getting a photo close-up by feeding one of our cute chipmunks or squirrels might seem like a good idea, but these animals have sharp teeth and might spread infection if they're sick. Fleas carried by ground squirrels have also been known to spread disease.

In fact, federal law now prohibits people from feeding or approaching any of our wildlife, and for good reason. The animals may look harmless, but most are capable of causing injury, and in extreme cases even death, to people who get too close. If an animal reacts to your presence, you're probably too close.

Besides, you can learn more about animal habits through quiet observation than interaction. For good photographs of animals in the woods, check the selection of postcards in the gift shop and books in the visitor center.

What animals are the most dangerous?

Yep, you guessed it: the chipmunks. Okay, maybe it wasn't your first guess; but nevertheless, the same cute little critters you try to feed and photograph have the distinction of being Muir Woods's most notorious biters. They're especially ornery when people try to lure them by pretending to have food, just to get a good picture. No food equals angry chipmunk. Angry chipmunk equals snapshot of someone who just had a finger nipped. Year-round, the most dangerous animal in Muir Woods is whichever one you try to feed.

The really dangerous animals that once roamed the woods, such as grizzly and black bears, were hunted out of the area long ago. Recently, we have seen the return of mountain lions in the higher areas of the park. Although they naturally avoid contact with humans, if you do see one of these animals, here are three tips:

1. **Don't run.** Fleeing often triggers a natural instinct in the animal to pursue.

2. **Make yourself look formidable.** Let the animal know you mean business.

3. **Hang onto children.** Kids may think it's fun to run out of your sight and unknowingly into the animal's territory.

The other creatures to watch out for are the coyote, who appears to be unafraid of people, and the Steller's jay, who is not shy about taking food right out of people's hands—or even mouths. Most injuries in the woods result from people getting too close to animals. The moral is, don't be fooled into thinking the cute little ones are harmless. Any animal that begs for food is potentially dangerous. Let's just say it's best if people and animals in the woods maintain a long-distance relationship.

Are there any great birding spots?

Although redwood forests are more famous for trees than for birds, Muir Woods has more than its share of feathered residents. Throughout the year, fifty species of birds call the woods home. They range in size from the tiny winter wren to an occasional great blue heron. For more information on seasonal birds in the woods, see the chart on page 47.

Avid birders have a vast array of interesting birds and birding areas to choose from outside the boundaries of Muir Woods. Let's start in the Marin Headlands, just beyond the north end of the Golden Gate Bridge and about 12 miles from the woods. For some awesome hawk-watching, try Hawk Hill during the annual fall migration, when thousands of hawks fly over the headlands, going south on the Pacific Coast flyway. The five-month season (August–December) peaks in September and October, when you'll see nineteen species of raptors—as many as 2,800 a day—flying overhead. For more information, call the Golden Gate Raptor Observatory at (415) 331-0730, or Hawkwatch Hotline at (415) 561-3030 ext. 2500.

In the Rodeo Valley area of the Marin Headlands, favorite birdwatching haunts include Rodeo Lagoon and Bird Island. From Rodeo Beach, you'll see lots of year-round cormorants and seagulls vying for space on the jagged crags of Bird Island. During the summer and early winter, brown pelicans arrive in droves, with up to 1,200 of these great brown birds settling on the rocks of the island at one time. One of the best pelican-watching locations on the West Coast is Clifftop Trail, overlooking the beach and island. The shallow wetlands of Rodeo Lagoon are a favorite feeding ground for egrets, ducks, and other shorebirds. For more information call the Marin Headlands Visitor Center at (415) 331-1540.

West of Muir Woods along Coast Highway 1 is Bolinas Lagoon, one of the best birdwatching areas in the Golden Gate National Recreation Area. The quiet waters, marshes, and mud flats of the lagoon host a diverse collection of year-round birds and wildlife that can easily be seen from roadside turnouts along Highway 1. Snowy egrets, black-birds, warblers, kingfishers, and cormorants are just some of the species you'll see all year. Seasonal residents include ducks in winter, great blue herons in spring, pelicans in summer, and sparrows in fall.

BIRD CHECKLIST: SU = summer, F = fall, W = winter, SP = spring. Darker boxes = greater abundance.

SU F W SP		SU F W SP		SU F W SP	
	Great Blue Heron		Pacific-slope Flycatcher		Ruby-crowned Kinglet
	Mallard		Olive-sided Flycatcher		Hutton's Vireo
	Turkey Vulture		Violet-green Swallow		Solitary Vireo
	Sharp-shinned Hawk		Barn Swallow		Warbling Vireo
	Red-tailed Hawk		Steller's Jay		Orange-crowned Warbler
	Cooper's Hawk		Scrub Jay		Townsend's Warbler
	American Kestrel		Common Raven		Wilson's Warbler
	California Quail		American Crow		Yellow Warbler
	Band-tailed Pigeon		Chestnut-backed		Hooded Warbler
	Rock Dove		Chickadee		Western Meadowlark
	Mourning Dove		Bushtit		Brewer's Blackbird
	Great Horned Owl		Wrentit		Black-headed Grosbeak
	Spotted Owl		American Dipper		Purple Finch
	Northern Saw-whet Owl		Pygmy Nuthatch		House Finch
	Anna's Hummingbird		Red-breasted Nuthatch		Pine Siskin
	Allen's Hummingbird		Brown Creeper		Red Crossbill
	Belted Kingfisher		Winter Wren		Rufous-sided Towhee
	Northern Flicker		Bewick's Wren		California Towhee
	Pileated Woodpecker		American Robin		Dark-eyed Junco
	Acorn Woodpecker		Varied Thrush		White-crowned Sparrow
	Red-breasted Sapsucker		Hermit Thrush		Golden-crowned Sparrow
	Hairy Woodpecker		Swainson's Thrush		Fox Sparrow
	Downy Woodpecker		Western Bluebird		Song Sparrow
	Black Phoebe		Golden-crowned Kinglet		House Sparrow

Audubon Canyon Ranch is a nonprofit, private 1,000-acre wildlife sanctuary on Bolinas Lagoon. During the spring more than 100 pairs of snowy egrets and great blue herons nest in the tops of the redwoods on the ranch. If you're here in May or June you might see adults teaching their young to fly and to fish in the lagoon. The ranch also has a nature education center with limited visiting hours and several miles of trails that are open to the public from mid-March to mid-July. Call the ranch office at (415) 868-9244 for more information.

North of Muir Woods on Highway 1, a small wildlife sanctuary on Tomales Bay hosts a variety of shorebirds, wading birds, and waterfowl, which are easily viewed along a nature trail through bay wetlands habitat. This is part of the Golden Gate National Recreational Area, and you get there from a large turnout on Highway 1 north of the town of Point Reyes Station. Watch for the sign. For more information, call the Bear Valley Visitor Center at (415) 663-1092.

Bird Checklist on page 47 by Carole Thickstun, from *The Muir Woods Map and Guide to Trails, Plants, and Wildlife*, published by the Golden Gate National Parks Association; used with permission.

Enough about animals. What kinds of plants will we see?

It takes a special kind of plant to survive the shade and moisture of a redwood forest. In Muir Woods, you'll discover a unique mosaic of varying shapes, sizes, and textures of plant life. As you walk through the woods, see how many of our forest plants you can identify.

One of our most common plants is the sword fern. With its long, sharp-pointed leaflets, which stay green year-round, it flourishes throughout the canyon in either single clumps or huge groups covering entire banks. You'll find all varieties of ferns here, including bracken ferns with large lacy triangles of flat leaves, lady ferns delicately lining the stream banks, and licorice ferns growing on trees during our moist months.

Plants that carpet the forest floor include Oregon oxalis (redwood sorrel), which resembles a small, delicate three-leafed clover, and wild ginger with large, leathery, heart-shaped leaves that form mats close to the ground. The oxygen-rich forest gives rise to moss and lichen, which cover rocks and tree trunks with lush coats of green, and shelf fungi, which grow on both living and dead trees. In the wet season, abundant fungi and mushrooms magically appear throughout the forest.

Along creeks, look for tall elk clover, with distinctive 5-by-7-inch leaves, from spring through fall. Fields of primitive horsetails, the oldest plant species in the woods, thrive year-round along Redwood Creek. Other plants include California hazel, a shrub that produces filbert nuts, which are an important food source for forest animals; huckleberry, with dark green leaves, white bell-shaped flowers in the spring, and berries in the fall; and western azalea, a large deciduous shrub that produces showy, fragrant yellow and white flowers. Recently, we've discovered rhododendrons growing in the woods. For more information on plants, see the books listed in Further Reading on page 129.

- Age studies of fire scars indicate that, prior to the arrival of Europeans, natural wildfires occurred in the Marin County area several times a century. During the last 150 years, humans have suppressed fire, interrupting the natural cycle of burning and regrowth. The last major fire in Muir Woods took place in the 1850s.
- You'll see evidence of ancient fires in the scars at the bases of large redwoods as you walk through the woods. These fire scars provide important habitat for wildlife, including "caves" for bats.
- Without fire, dead wood and leaf litter accumulate to create unnatural fire hazards. Frequent, low-intensity fires actually decrease the danger of large, uncontrollable wildfires.
- Besides the obvious damage to private property and land, high-intensity, uncontrollable wildfires also damage the soil by heating the ground so that it becomes impermeable to water, and winter rains don't percolate through the earth. This creates a situation that endangers plants, soil, and downslope areas, as increased runoff results in erosion and potential flooding.
- In 1997, the NPS instituted a program of prescribed burning in the Muir Woods area to reduce fuels and help create natural fire breaks. These planned and carefully controlled fires are set only when specific conditions of soil moisture, fuel moisture, wind direction, wind speed, temperature, and humidity are met. During the burn, the weather, flame height, length, and rate of spread of the fire are monitored regularly. Controlled burns are planned for designated days and times to minimize impact on the surrounding communities and meet all requirements of local health and safety codes.
- Benefits from prescribed burns include:
  ⇨ Encouraging mineral recycling in the soil by turning dead wood and other debris into ash.
  ⇨ Establishing an edge in the vegetation that creates a beneficial wildlife habitat.
  ⇨ Clearing understory debris without killing mature trees, which helps to control forest insects and diseases.
  ⇨ Opening up the forest to more light.
  ⇨ Encouraging the successional development of many plant communities, including the coast redwood, which relies on fire to make conditions optimal for seed germination. Other trees and shrubs in redwood, oak woodland, and chaparral areas also regenerate after fire, through vigorous growth of crown and root sprouts.
- During a prescribed burn, visitors to the area usually have to use alternative hiking and biking routes as posted at the trailheads. Once the area is safe, tours are conducted so you can see the burn for yourself. For more information on prescribed burns, call the Muir Woods Ranger Station at (415) 388-2596.

Where are the best places to see wildflowers?

The low light of Muir Woods may not produce the greatest display of wildflowers, but blooms do start in January and last throughout the fall. Let's wander through this ten-month season to discover one of the woods' best-kept secrets: forest wildflowers.

Winter: If you're here in January, you may have to hunt for the first flower to bloom in the woods: the fetid adder's-tongue. You can identify it by the three petals making the shape of a tongue or by catching a whiff of its rank smell. In February, throughout the woods you'll find the pale California toothwort, commonly called rainbells, blue iris, and hound's-tongue, a deep bluish purple with long tongue-shaped leaves.

Western Hounds Tongue

Spring: In meadows, along stream banks, and by trails and roadsides, forest wildflowers begin their spring show in March, as the woods dry out from winter's rain. Look for three-leafed trilliums, including the western wake-robin, with large green leaves and blossoms that slowly change from white to lavender as the season progresses. Other early bloomers include the pale pink, clover-shaped Oregon oxalis and the lemon-yellow redwood violet. In May and June, the bright pink blooms of clintonia, starflower, and fairy lantern dot the woods, the California buckeye tree sports profuse whitish-pink blossoms, and the small white flowers of miner's lettuce bloom throughout the lower canyon.

Western Wake Robin

Summer: As the days lengthen, look for masses of creamy, fragrant blooms on azalea bushes along Redwood Creek and the tall white flowers of cow parsnip on the forest floor. One of the last plants to bloom in the woods is elk clover, or California aralia, whose tall stalks burst into clusters of tiny white flowers in August. The berries that follow darken as they mature. Elderberries, thimbleberries, and huckleberries tempt the birds with red fruit.

Fall: Many of the forest wildflowers continue to bloom well into September and October. Then, as the amount of daylight in the forest decreases with the season, our flowers end their blooming for the year. Look for buckeye fruits hanging on their now-leafless branches, acorns dropping from oaks, and any hazelnuts the squirrels have missed.

Outside Muir Woods: Wildflower hunting is at its best in the meadows of the upper trails, especially the Ocean View and Sun Trails, and in the rolling hills and meadowlands of the Marin Headlands, which offer a vast array of wildflower habitats and species. The Point Bonita Lighthouse, Tennessee Valley, Coastal, Wolf Ridge, and Miwok Trails are all worth a try.

Checkerbloom

Can we see fall color in the woods?

Compared to some places, there's not much color to see in this land of evergreens. But the best time for fall color in Muir Woods is, naturally, the fall. By late September, the fog starts to recede, and warm hues fill Redwood Canyon. The change of season is subtle here, so you won't see the forest ignite in a spectacular display, but it does put on its own kind of fall show, when we enjoy our warmest temperatures of the year. We consider it nature's harvest time—one of my favorite seasons in the woods. Here are some things to look for:

- ➪ Bigleaf maples accent the silence of the forest with splashes of color, and their golden leaves drift gracefully to the forest floor. Red alder leaves intermingle with the maples', leaving a coat of fall color on the ground and in the quiet waters of Redwood Creek.

- ➪ Poison oak vines turn a bright red, as if ablaze throughout the forest, in an otherwise soft-hued season.

- ➪ Red ladybugs cluster on the horsetail ferns near Redwood Creek and along forest trails.

- ➪ Orange-and-black monarch butterflies flutter through the woods in their annual migration toward milder weather.

- ➪ Redwood needles turn brown and rain down on the forest floor.

- ➪ Brown buckeye pods fall to the ground.

- ➪ Crayfish, in hues of red and blue, creep in creek pools.

- ➪ Aralia berries ripen and turn black.

- ➪ The tanbark oaks drop their brown acorns for harvesting by forest squirrels and chipmunks.

For more information about changing seasons in the woods, or for other areas throughout the GGNRA where you can see fall color, check out the books in Further Reading on pages 129–130.

Of all the plants that grow in the woods, the one to watch out for the most has the deadly name poison oak. It's not lethal, but a bad case of poison oak can be very nasty. Distinguished by its three oaklike leaves and slightly down-curved edges, this plant grows mostly in sunny areas along our hillside trails. The problem is, it grows in many forms: as a small weed, as a vine climbing up a redwood, and as a large bush. In any form, its oil is highly toxic to humans and produces an intensely itchy skin rash that can last from a few days to two weeks. The plant is easily identified in the fall when its leaves turn bright red, unlike our other plants, which remain green. Although visitors find it harmful, poison oak does provide an important food source for many animals in the woods.

The stinging nettle is another plant that you should avoid brushing against. Mostly found along hillside trails and meadows above the redwood groves, its sturdy stalks and soft leaves can prick and irritate your skin, causing hours of discomfort.

Our trees are generally visitor-friendly, but there are certain situations in which you need to take precautions. In a strong wind, tree branches sometimes break and fall to the forest floor, a potentially rude surprise if you're walking on the trail below. Although it doesn't happen very often, trees have toppled in the woods, especially those weakened by age or fire. The best advice is, if you're here on a particularly windy day, remain alert, and keep an eye out for falling branches. If a tree is about to fall, you'll probably hear it in plenty of time to get out of its path. And it will give you a good story to tell.

What's that plant?

Poison Oak!

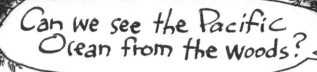

Can we see the Pacific Ocean from the woods?

Only if you have the time to reach the higher-elevation trails. You'll have to hike up out of Muir Woods to get the best vistas of the ocean. Even Ocean View Trail (also called Panoramic Trail) does not live up to its name. It used to provide great ocean views, but that was before the forest grew up and blocked vistas to the coast.

You'll find the start of Ocean View Trail on the right from the Main Loop Trail just after the visitor center. The trail is steep in parts but mostly consists of gentle climbs all the way to Panoramic Highway. As you walk up the slope, you'll experience the range of plant life on Mount Tamalpais: redwoods in the canyons, tanbark oak, madrone, and Douglas fir at the middle elevations, and chaparral at the top.

Here are two options for hikes that start in Muir Woods:

For some of the best ocean viewing in the GGNRA, your best bet is to take the Ben Johnson Trail, along Deer Park Ridge Trail, to the Dipsea which takes you back to Muir Woods in about 3.5 hours and offers an eyeful of the mighty Pacific.

For a longer hike, take Ocean View Trail for 1.5 miles, then turn right on Redwood Trail, a 1.7-mile trek with great views of the ocean and Muir Woods. This hike brings you to the Tourist Club for some well-deserved refreshments. To go back to Muir Woods, take the Sun Trail loop (instead of the steeper Muir Woods Trail), cross Muir Woods Road, and then catch the Dipsea Trail back to the woods. It's a half-day, 5.2-mile round trip that will reward you with some excellent ocean vistas.

The best way to avoid the crowds at Muir Woods is to come in the spring, fall, or winter, on weekdays, or in the early mornings and late afternoons of summer. If you just can't avoid our rush hours, then the next best thing is to hike up one of the trails that go out of the woods. Since 98 percent of our visitors stay on the Main Loop Trail in the canyon, you can lose the crowd by taking the less frequented, higher-elevation trails.

Some of the trails you might want to consider are Fern Creek, Ben Johnson, Redwood Creek, or Dipsea. Be sure to check at the visitor center for trail length, conditions, and closures, and make sure you know which route will bring you back to the woods. It's important to take water, snacks, layered clothing, a map, and a compass. Make sure you pick a trail that matches your stamina and respects your past injuries. For more information about hiking in and around Muir Woods, refer to pages 62–70.

How can we take great pictures of the woods?

Y ou may get lucky with one of those disposable cameras, but for postcard-quality photos of Muir Woods, you'll probably need better equipment. A wide-angle lens can help you capture the height of the trees. The light is often dim, so either bring a tripod for making long exposures or use fast film or a digital camera with fast-speed capability. A polarizing filter can deepen color but requires a longer exposure. A flash is useful if you plan on taking close-up shots.

For a top-to-bottom picture of a redwood, the trees at the entrance of the parking lot are the most cooperative models. Within the woods, Cathedral Grove has some beauties, and the best time to snap photos of them is usually in the early morning, before the crowds arrive. Sometimes it helps to have a person in the picture next to the trees, to provide a reference for their awesome scale. Don't fret about overcast skies; they may provide the most even light. And consider capturing details, such as the time-worn grooves in the bark or a sunlit fern. Always remember to stay on boardwalks and paths.

Every season offers a different scene for photographers. Summer brings the creeping coastal fog, which hangs in the canyon. To capture it, you might want to shoot from the road to Mount Tamalpais, well above Muir Woods. Autumn offers splashes of color in the turning trees, and often there's a mellow haze in the air that acts as a natural filter. Late autumn rains make the woods glisten and sprout mushrooms. Deer occasionally appear, and fish come upstream to spawn, though they're often hidden in the storm-churned water. A low sun angle can produce striking rays of light through the trees. The transition from winter to spring offers a chance to chronicle intrepid flowers, bright new leaves on the alders and maples, and ferns unfurling their fiddleheads to the world.

I owe special thanks to Muir Woods photographer James M. Morley for sharing his experience and expertise with me. You can pick up a copy of his beautiful book, *Muir Woods: The Ancient Redwood Forest near San Francisco*, at the visitor center.

> # What can we take home as a memento of our visit?

With Muir Woods as a backdrop, anyone with a camera can take home some of the magic without stealing anything from the beauty of the woods. There are no mementos quite like the photographs that capture and give life to your own special memories, such as an autumn walk through the giant redwoods or a hike up Ben Johnson Trail to a spectacular view of the Pacific Ocean.

For less adventuresome keepsakes, check out the gift shop and the visitor center bookstore. Besides the ever-popular T-shirts and mugs, the gift shop offers a wide range of mementos that evoke the spirit of Muir Woods, including living redwood tree sprouts and a seedling/seed kit (both $6.99); live redwood burls ($3.99 to $6.99); redwood jewelry; locally crafted redwood vases, boxes, and bowls; hand-carved redwood figures ($15.50 to $444); a carved wall hanging of a redwood grove ($400), small redwood wall trees ($18.99 to $27), and miniature redwood tree magnets ($4.99). In the visitor center bookstore you'll find native plant seeds, glue slugs, audiotapes, and the best selection of Muir Woods books anywhere.

The search for souvenirs can become a problem in Muir Woods. That's why people are prohibited from destroying or removing just about everything in the woods, including plants, animals, minerals, and archaeological artifacts. A family walking out with a basketful of redwood cones shouldn't be surprised if the ranger hands out a $50 to $100 citation—one of the less desirable mementos of Muir Woods. These regulations are designed to keep Muir Woods intact despite the 1.8 million visitors per year who want to take a piece of it home.

Recreational Opportunities

What's there to do around here?

With all the action in Muir Woods, Mount Tamalpais State Park, the Marin Headlands, and the rest of the enormous Golden Gate National Recreation Area, you'll never be without some form of year-round outdoor recreation. Let's take a look at the possibilities.

HIKING AND WALKING

The 6 miles of trails in Muir Woods are surrounded by 60 miles of some of the best year-round hiking and walking in the world. How many places on earth can offer a blanket of spring wildflowers, whales breaching off shore in summer, a winter walk amid giant redwoods, and a crystal autumn view of San Francisco? For those who want a more rigorous, several-day adventure, we have trails that lead to picturesque inns, where you can rest up for exploring some of the most beautiful landscapes and vistas in California. For more information on hikes in and around Muir Woods, refer to pages 62–70.

MOUNTAIN BIKING & HORSEBACK RIDING

Neither mountain bikes nor horses are allowed within Muir Woods, but that still leaves miles of well-maintained fire roads throughout the GGNRA. Rolling past spectacular vistas and through tranquil groves, mountain bikers can explore the same scenic paths where the sport was invented in the 1970s. Horseback riders can travel our fire roads and designated trails in the same mode of transportation as the area's first visitors. Although the pace on a horse is slower than on a two-wheeler, you have the advantage of being higher in the saddle to catch

a better glimpse of our more elusive wildlife, such as bobcats. For more information, refer to page 71 (mountain bikes) or page 72 (horses).

WATER RECREATION

Although you'll never hear "surf's up" in Muir Woods, there are plenty of opportunities for swimming, surfing, body boarding, and skim boarding at area beaches, including Muir, Rodeo, and Stinson, during the late summer months when the water is warmer. Canoeists and kayakers can paddle several inland waterways within the GGNRA. For more information on water recreation areas, refer to pages 78–79.

FISHING

You can't wet a line in the woods, but the fishing is good in other areas of the GGNRA. Try Stinson or Muir Beach for some rigorous surf fishing. For a quieter experience, cast your line in one of the lakes in north Marin, such as Bon Tempe, Phoenix, Alpine, Lagunitas, or Kent Lakes. For more information, refer to page 73.

BEACHCOMBING

The Pacific Coast near Muir Woods is a beachcomber's paradise. The coastal areas and beaches north of the Golden Gate Bridge to Point Reyes National Seashore offer a treasure trove of surfside activities—collecting mussels at Muir Beach, exploring the tide pools at Slide Ranch, or enjoying a picnic above Kirby Cove. For more information, refer to pages 78–79.

CAMPING

The area around Muir Woods offers thirteen campgrounds for spending the night in the great outdoors: four drive-to campgrounds, five hike-in backpack camps, and four group camps, including one for equestrians. Amenities range from primitive campsites with pit toilets to a full-service campground with RV hookups and a laundromat. For more information, refer to pages 74–77.

How much of Muir Woods is accessible to hikers?

Within Muir Woods, there are 6 miles of trails, which mostly follow the perimeter boundary and waterways of the woods. These include the Muir Woods, Hillside, and Ben Johnson Trails, and segments of the Dipsea and Deer Park Trails. The Fern Creek, Ocean View, and Stapelveldt Trails start in Muir Woods, then lead out of the canyon to higher-elevation routes.

The trails that stick to the woods provide an easy to moderately easy hiking experience. For diverse terrain mixed with ocean and city views, your best choice is to walk up Hillside from the Main Loop Trail in Redwood Canyon, then hike up Ben Johnson to Dipsea, which will bring you back to the entrance after 3.5 miles.

For more adventuresome hikes, you can take off in literally any direction on the more than 60 miles of Mount Tamalpais trails surrounding Muir Woods. These longer routes traverse unique landscapes and habitats that have made the area a mecca for day hikers and overnight campers. See pages 68–70 for recommended hikes. *Tamalpais Trails*, by Barry Spitz, offers a good overview of the trails and natural history of the area.

A word of advice about hiking the longer trails: make sure you're prepared with water, snacks, personal items, extra clothes, and a map and compass (and the know-how to use them). One of my favorite trail maps, *A Rambler's Guide to the Trails of Mt. Tamalpais and the Marin Headlands*, is available at the visitor center. It's always a good idea to check with a ranger at the visitor center for an update on trail conditions before you start.

What do we need to know about hiking in and around Muir Woods?

First, a bit of history. From old summit hiking registers, we know that people came to hike Mount Tamalpais's awesome terrain in the late 1800s, establishing the mountain as a favorite hiking destination for locals and visitors alike. The Sierra Club, founded by John Muir, organized its first Tam hike in 1902, and ten years later the Tamalpais Conservation Club (TCC) began maintaining Tam trails, adopting the motto "Guardian of the Mountain." Other hiking organizations, including the Tourist Club and the California Alpine Club, established early clubhouses on Mount Tamalpais. So when you hike the trails in and around Muir Woods, you're carrying on a tradition that began more than 100 years ago.

Fortunately, our rich hiking history has also taught us which precautions you should take to make your trek an enjoyable and memorable experience.

Measuring only 1/8 inch long, the hard-to-see western black-legged tick is a year-round pest that can, on rare occasions, cause Lyme disease if imbedded in human skin for a length of time. Check yourself after hiking trips, remove any ticks carefully, and consult a doctor if the area shows signs of infection (a circular, reddish rash). Other critters to watch out for include various species of bees and yellow jackets, which have a nasty habit of invading summer picnics. If you get severe reactions to their stings, include an allergy kit in your backpack. The mountain is also home to the western rattlesnake, which should always be given a wide berth. Although the chance of seeing a mountain lion is remote, several sightings have been reported on Mount Tam in recent years. Look for warning signs of recent sightings at trailheads, and refer to page 45 for more information.

Black-legged ticks...
Rattlesnakes...
Poison oak...
Deadly mushrooms...

Poison oak is abundant on Mount Tam, and its oil can cause a reaction in humans that ranges from mild to extreme inflammation and irritation of the skin. Steer clear of any plants with leaves of three. Even in winter, when it loses its foliage, it's toxic; so, if you think you've touched the plant, do yourself a favor and wash with Fels Naphtha soap, or apply Tecnu cleanser, as soon as possible after exposure. With hundreds of colorful mushroom species growing in the wet, forested areas of Muir Woods, it's tempting for people pick them—even the deadly ones. Harvesting mushrooms is now tightly controlled to protect visitors from eating potentially poisonous species.

Although Mount Tamalpais has no documented cases of giardiasis, an intestinal ailment caused by drinking untreated water, it's best not to take chances. Carry an adequate supply of drinking water (one or two quarts per person) on any hike.

Since lightning is rare on Mount Tamalpais, most fires in the area are caused by humans. Use extreme caution regarding potential fire-causing activities such as smoking or making a campfire, using a barbecue, or lighting fireworks, especially during the hot, dry months of summer and fall. Call (415) 499-7191 for daily updates on fire conditions and trail and road closures.

Can we take a ranger-led walk?

Follow me.

The best way to unlock the secrets of Muir Woods is to hang out with the people who have the keys: the rangers and volunteer interpretive guides.

Guides offer fifteen-minute orientation talks every hour on the half-hour. Groups can arrange guided walks through Redwood Canyon with a ranger or interpretive guide and even request specific guides known for their expertise and vivid interpretive talks. Rangers from Muir Woods also lead Muir Beach tidepool explorations and give military history talks at Muir Beach Overlook. Call the visitor center at (415) 388-2595 for more information.

Longer ranger-led hikes take visitors up out of the canyon to dramatic watershed views, areas of historic interest, and trails that explore wildlife migratory habits. Here's a rundown on what you'll see on these hikes:

<u>WATERSHED VIEW HIKES</u>
You can take a half-day ranger-led hike (3.5 hours) that starts at the visitor center and travels up Ben Johnson Trail, along Deer Park Ridge Trail and down into the woods on the Dipsea Trail. Along the way you'll learn about the various plant communities found throughout the Redwood Creek watershed, view prescribed-burn and field research areas, and enjoy breathtaking views of the Pacific Ocean and San Francisco. It's also not unusual to see raptors and bobcats on this hike.

For a longer hike, join a ranger on a full-day trek (5 hours) that explores the many areas of the watershed and offers expansive ocean and city views. It starts at the visitor center, travels up Fern Creek Loop Trail and Ben Johnson Trail to Lone Tree Spring, explores the ridges of Coastal Trail through Kent Canyon, crosses the Heather cut-off, goes along Dias Ridge and Miwok Trails, and then follows Redwood Creek Trail back to Muir Woods. You'll need to bring plenty of water and your own lunch.

MIGRATION HIKE

If you've ever wanted to follow the trail of migrating animals, then join a ranger for this full-day hike (4.5 to 5 hours), which starts at the visitor center and follows the spawning salmon and steelhead along Redwood Creek into Frank's Valley and Terwilliger Grove. This excursion offers a chance to see raptors along the Pacific Flyway, gray whales off Muir Beach, and waterfowl nesting in the Monterey pines and cypresses nearby. If you go during the fall, you may even see thousands of monarch butterflies clustering in the trees that surround Muir Beach.

"WALK INTO THE PAST" HIKE

For history buffs, this half-day ranger-led hike (3.5 to 4 hours) travels along one of the oldest Indian trading routes in the area and explores other points of historic interest. Starting on Panoramic Highway at the Mountain Home Inn, you'll travel down the historic Camp Alice Eastwood Grade, through Muir Woods, along the famous Dipsea Trail to Deer Park Trail, then across the TCC Trail to Troop 80 Trail and back to the Mountain Home Inn. As you explore the routes, you'll learn the origins of these trails.

For more information on ranger-led hike schedules, call the visitor center at (415) 388-2596. The Mount Tamalpais Interpretive Association sponsors hikes for the public on a wide range of subjects year-round. These hikes are led by knowledgeable association members. Call (415) 258-2410 or 388-2070 for more information. To find out about similar hikes given in the Marin Headlands call (415) 331-1540, or for hikes in the Point Reyes National Seashore call (415) 663-1092.

> **What should we take on our day hike?**

HERE'S A RUNDOWN ON DAY HIKING ESSENTIALS IN SUMMER:

Clothing: Start with a pair of lightweight boots, hiking shoes, or sturdy, comfortable sneakers with good traction. Because of ticks and poison oak, I recommend long pants. If the weather changes you'll be glad to have pants made of material that dries quickly, such as nylon, nylon/cotton blend, or light wool. A long-sleeved polyester shirt and a polyester/fleece vest or wool sweater allow for layering, and a water-proof, wind-proof shell with attached hood can protect you against moist fog and nasty weather. Bring along a rain suit, if you have one, and pack a warm hat to keep your head dry and prevent heat loss if the weather changes.

Equipment: A small daypack, knapsack, or fanny pack and plenty of water are essential, especially in warm weather and on long hikes. Snacks are a good idea, particularly when hungry children are along for the hike. Whatever you bring, remember to pack out all your trash. Other essentials include insect repellent, sunscreen, lip balm, sunglasses, and a first-aid kit (or just a few bandages to take care of any scrapes and cuts). Sometimes a hike lasts longer than you expect; instead of having to find your way back in the dark, pack a flashlight.

Bathrooms are scarce once you're away from the visitor area in Muir Woods, so carry toilet paper with you. Human waste must be buried at least 6 inches deep, 100 feet or more from any water or trail. A small trowel helps.

Depending on your interests, you can bring along other items to add to your adventure, such as field books, binoculars, and a camera. A map, compass, knife, and police whistle and the know-how to use them can be useful tools.

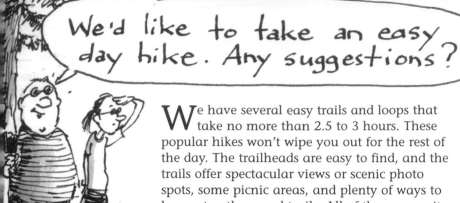

We'd like to take an easy day hike. Any suggestions?

We have several easy trails and loops that take no more than 2.5 to 3 hours. These popular hikes won't wipe you out for the rest of the day. The trailheads are easy to find, and the trails offer spectacular views or scenic photo spots, some picnic areas, and plenty of ways to hop onto other good trails. All of them are suitable for families with children. All distances are for round trips.

HIKE	TIME/DISTANCE	DIFFICULTY	STARTS FROM
MAIN LOOP TRAIL to Cathedral Grove	1 hour/1 mile	easy	Visitor center
MAIN LOOP TRAIL to Hillside Trail	1.5 hours/2 miles	easy	Visitor center
FERN CREEK TRAIL TO CAMP ALICE EASTWOOD	2 hours/3 miles	easy	Visitor center
MUIR WOODS ROAD TO REDWOOD CREEK TRAIL TO MUIR BEACH	2.5 hours/6 miles	easy/moderate	Lower parking lot
GRAVITY CAR GRADE TO OLD RAILROAD GRADE & HOGBACK TRAIL	2 hours/2.6 miles	easy/moderate	Mountain Home Inn
ALPINE TRAIL TO BOOTJACK TRAIL TO EASY GRADE TRAIL TO OLD STAGE ROAD	2 hours/2 miles	easy/moderate	Pan Toll

How about some more challenging hikes?

These trails are a bit tougher than the easy hikes, requiring more time or a little more oomph to walk up some moderate slopes and occasional steep parts. Families with children are welcome to have a go; just make sure you have plenty of water and snacks. Many of these treks will lead you to awesome scenery, great picnic spots, and points of historic interest. All distances are for round trips.

HIKE	TIME/DISTANCE	DIFFICULTY	STARTS FROM
MAIN LOOP TRAIL TO BOOTJACK TRAIL TO TCC TRAIL TO BEN JOHNSON TRAIL BACK TO THE LOOP TRAIL	3.5 hours/6 miles	moderate	Visitor center
OCEAN VIEW TRAIL TO REDWOOD TRAIL TO SUN TRAIL	3 hours/5.2 miles	moderate	Visitor center
MAIN LOOP TRAIL TO OCEAN VIEW TRAIL TO LOST TRAIL TO FERN CREEK TRAIL	2.5 hours/3.1 miles	moderate	Visitor center
HOGBACK TRAIL TO MATT DAVIS TRAIL TO NORA TRAIL TO WEST POINT TRAIL TO OLD RAILROAD GRADE TO HOGBACK TRAIL	3 hours/4 miles	moderate+	Mountain Home Inn
OLD STAGE ROAD TO OLD MINE TRAIL TO ROCK SPRING TRAIL PAST MOUNTAIN THEATER TO WEST POINT, THEN TO OLD STAGE ROAD	3+ hours/4.5 miles	moderate+	Pan Toll

What are some great butt-kicking hikes?

For those who like to get their hearts really pumping and feel the burn in their legs, here's a list of some trails that will happily oblige. You'll need to be in good shape and carefully plan your trip for these babies, but they'll pay you back with some spectacular scenery and vistas, a few pools and waterfalls, and a feeling of accomplishment once you're finished. Most of these can be done in a day, but you may want to rest in picnic areas along the way. Just be sure you have the time and energy before embarking on these journeys, as most have strenuous uphill climbs, some creek crossings, and higher elevations, which mean that much more huffing and puffing. Distances are for round trips.

HIKE	TIME/DISTANCE	DIFFICULTY	STARTS FROM
MAIN LOOP TRAIL TO BEN JOHNSON TRAIL TO DIPSEA TRAIL TO STINSON BEACH, RETURN VIA STEEP RAVINE AND STAPELVELDT TRAILS	6 hours/10 miles	moderate/strenuous	Visitor center
MATT DAVIS TRAIL TO COASTAL TRAIL TO CATARACT TRAIL	4 hours/6.6 miles	moderate/strenuous	Pan Toll
MATT DAVIS TRAIL TO STINSON BEACH	4+ hours/7 miles	strenuous	Pan Toll
MUIR WOODS ROAD TO REDWOOD CREEK TRAIL TO MIWOK TRAIL TO COYOTE RIDGE TRAIL TO GREEN GULCH TRAIL, RETURN VIA REDWOOD CREEK TRAIL	5 hours/7.5 miles	strenuous	Lower parking lot
CATARACT TRAIL TO HIGH MARSH TO KENT TRAIL TO HELEN MARKT TRAIL	5 hours/ 7.7 miles	strenuous	Alpine Dam

Can we mountain bike in Muir Woods?

Although you can't ride anywhere in Muir Woods, mountain bikes are allowed on grades, paved roads, and fire roads that surround the woods. You just can't ride on any trails.

As a matter of fact, mountain biking was invented on Mount Tamalpais in the 1970s, with the first models tested on the mountain's fire roads. Therefore, the *mountain* in *mountain bike* refers to Tamalpais. Now, these fat-tired, multi-geared two-wheelers have become world-famous ways to enjoy off-road recreation.

Because of the growing popularity and numbers of mountain bikes on paved and fire roads in the area, their use is becoming controversial. The speed limit is 15 miles per hour, 5 miles per hour on curves or when passing. For a bike trail map, information, and updates on local mountain biking issues, contact the Marin Bicycle Trails Council at (415) 456-7512.

Can we go horseback riding?

Since the arrival of European settlers in the 1830s, horses have been a popular means of travel and recreation in the areas surrounding Muir Woods. Beginning in the 1890s, tourists rented horses and donkeys to take them to favorite picnic spots in and around the woods or hired horse-drawn stagecoaches to travel across Mount Tamalpais to oceanside retreats. The arrival of automobiles eclipsed horse transportation, but horseback riding remains a popular activity among equestrians in the area.

Although horses are not permitted in Muir Woods, they can use fire roads and some trails on Mount Tamalpais and most of the trails in the GGNRA surrounding the woods. Always check trailhead signs, as trails may be temporarily closed to horses due to seasonal conditions. You can also call the following offices to get updates on closures and conditions on riding trails within their respective areas: Mount Tamalpais State Park, (415) 388-2070; GGNRA, (415) 556-0560; Marin Headlands Visitor Center, (415) 331-1540; and Marin Municipal Water District Sky Oaks Ranger Station, (415) 459-5267.

Opened in 1990, the Frank's Valley Group Horse Camp is located on Muir Beach Road at Santos Meadow and can accommodate overnight stays for groups with two to twelve horses. For more information and reservations (required), call the Pan Toll Ranger Station at (415) 388-2070. For the nearest riding lessons, organized trail rides, hourly horse rentals, and even a summer horse camp for kids, call Miwok Livery Stables in Tennessee Valley in the Marin Headlands at (415) 383-8048, or try Five Brooks Ranch and Stables in the Point Reyes National Seashore at (415) 663-1570.

Are there any good fishing spots?

Anglers are not allowed to pursue their passion within Muir Woods, but don't worry; good fishing can be found within 3 miles of the woods. Try surf fishing for ocean perch at either Muir Beach (3 miles) or Stinson Beach (6 miles)—just make sure you have gear that can weather the pounding surf. You'll also find scenic angling in San Francisco Bay, on the fishing pier at East Fort Baker under the Golden Gate Bridge, where perch, flounder, smelt, salmon, and rock crab may be caught. If you have your own boat, you can launch it on the east side of Tomales Bay for some great salmon and halibut fishing.

For anglers who prefer fresh water, there are five fishable lakes located throughout the Tamalpais watershed—Alpine, Bon Tempe, Kent, Lagunitas, and Phoenix. All within easy drives from Muir Woods, these lakes are periodically stocked with bass and trout. Since the 1980s, Lake Lagunitas has been a self-sustaining trout fishery owing to new stocking methods and regulations: you can fish there only with artificial lures and single barbless hooks, and the limit is two fish measuring less than 14 inches. Phoenix Lake was drained in the 1980s, and 1,700 tires were placed on the lake bed to serve as breeding places for what is now a healthy population of largemouth bass.

All anglers over the age of sixteen need a valid California fishing license. Be sure to check and observe posted regulations. You can call the Marin Municipal Water District (MMWD) fishing hotline at (415) 459-0888 for more information and current lake-stocking schedules.

Whether you hike or drive, alone or with a group, you have a variety of camping alternatives within the boundaries of the GGNRA. Choices range from sleeping inside a historic army bunker overlooking the ocean to pitching your tent next to a stream in a redwood forest. Since all these sites are popular, it's best to call for reservations well in advance of your arrival. Refer to the map on page 77 for general locations of the numbered campgrounds.

DRIVE-TO CAMPGROUNDS

1. Pan Toll Campground is located near the summit of Mount Tamalpais above Muir Woods. From the parking lot you'll have a 100-yard walk to sixteen campsites with access to some of the best hiking trails on Mount Tamalpais. Facilities include flush toilets, picnic tables, barbecue grills, and water. Registration is on a first-come, first-served basis, and the cost is $16 per night (weekends), $15 (weekdays), from April through October, and $12 the rest of the year. You'll pay extra for dogs. Call (415) 388-2070 for more information.

2. Steep Ravine Environmental Campground lives up to its name with six primitive campsites and ten rustic cabins perched on a steep hill overlooking a cove and beach at Rocky Point, south of Stinson Beach. Facilities include pit toilets, picnic tables, barbecue grills, and water; cabins have wood-burning stoves. Cabin fees are $30 per night year-round, and campsites cost $11 (weekends), $10 (weekdays), from April through October, and $7 the rest of the year. Pets are not allowed. To make reservations (required), call (800) 444-7275. Insider's tip: If you cross Highway 1 from Steep Ravine and venture up Webb Creek on the Steep Ravine Trail, you'll find waterfalls and cascades in winter and an intimate redwood canyon hike year-round.

3. Olema Ranch Campground is located in Olema Valley near the beaches and trails of the Point Reyes National Seashore, just 2 miles south of Point Reyes Station on Highway 1. Facilities include RV hookups, tent sites, picnic tables, showers, flush toilets, laundromat, camp store, post office, propane, gas, clubhouse, and rental trailers. The cost is $25 per night for RVs, $20 for tents. There's a $3 per person charge for more than two people, and a $2 per vehicle charge for more than one vehicle. Dogs cost an extra $1. Registration is 8 a.m. to 8 p.m. Call (415) 663-8001 for more information and reservations (recommended April–October).

4. Samuel P. Taylor State Park offers sixty sites for RVs and tents in a redwood forest on the east side of Bolinas Ridge and Mount Tamalpais, 15 miles west of San Rafael on Sir Francis Drake Boulevard. Facilities include showers, flush toilets, picnic tables, barbecues, and water; there are no RV hookups. Sites cost $15 per night (weekends), $14 (weekdays), April–October, and $12 the rest of the year. Reservations are required April–September. Call (800) 444-7275 or (415) 488-9897 for more information.

HIKE-IN BACKPACK CAMPS

5. Hawk Backpack Camp in the Marin Headlands is accessed by the Bobcat (3.5-mile hike) or Marincello or Miwok Trails (3-mile trek) from the Tennessee Valley parking lot. It offers great Bay Area views plus three campsites for up to four people each, chemical toilets, and picnic tables. There's no water, and no fires are allowed. Sites are free, but reservations and permits are required. Call (415) 331-1540.

6. Haypress Backpack Camp is located at the end of a grassy section of the Tennessee Valley in the Marin Headlands. Access is from the parking lot for the Tennessee Valley trailhead, an easy 0.75-mile walk that's great for fami-

lies. For more strenuous hiking, you can take the Coyote Ridge Trail from Muir Beach. Facilities include five campsites for up to four people each, a chemical toilet, and picnic tables. No water is available, and fires are not allowed. One site is designed to accommodate wheelchairs. Reservations and permits are required. Call (415) 331-1540.

7. Bicentennial Camp offers three campsites (limit of two people per site) about 100 feet from Field Road in the Marin Headlands. You'll get some great ocean views, but facilities are spare—picnic tables and a chemical toilet. Call (415) 331-1540.

8. Glen Camp in the Point Reyes National Seashore is located in secluded woods between Inverness Ridge and the coast. It offers easy access to the beaches. The campsites have picnic tables, pit toilets, barbecue grills, and water. Access is a steep 5-mile hike from Five Brooks trailhead along Stewart Trail in the Olema Valley. Advance reservations and permits are required. Call (415) 663-8054 (9 a.m.–2 p.m. Monday through Friday).

9. Wildcat Camp is located on an oceanfront cliff north of Double Point in the Point Reyes National Seashore. It offers great beach and coastal views, group and individual campsites, picnic tables, pit toilets, barbecue grills, and water. Access is a steep 5.7-mile hike from Five Brooks trailhead along the Stewart Trail in Olema Valley, or from Palomarin and Bear Valley. Advance reservations and permits are required. Call (415) 663-8054 or (415) 663-1092 for information.

GROUP CAMPGROUNDS

10. Battery Alexander Group Camp is located in a historic military bunker in the Marin Headlands just south of Rodeo Lagoon. It offers sleeping areas indoors (in the bunker) and outdoors for year-round group camping. Other facilities include pit toilets, picnic tables, barbecue grills, and water. Drive-in access is available from Bunker and Field Roads. This area is for groups of fifteen to eighty people, and reservations and permits are required. The cost is $20 per night. Call (415) 561-4304.

11. Kirby Cove Group Camp is located in a picturesque cove and beach at the foot of the Golden Gate Bridge in the Marin Headlands. Available from April through October only, it offers bridge and city

skyline views, campsites for two to ten people, tent pads, fire pits, picnic tables, pit toilets, and barbecue grills. No water is available, and access is limited—it's best to drive or walk in from Conzelman Road. Reservations and permits are required, and there's a three-day maximum stay. The cost is $20 per night. Call (415) 561-4304.

12. Alice Eastwood Group Camp offers two campsites accommodating twenty-five to seventy-five people each in a wooded canyon north of Muir Woods. Besides access to great Mount Tamalpais trails, you'll find picnic tables, pit toilets, barbecue grills, and water. You can arrive by car or on foot from Panoramic Highway. Reservations and permits are required. Call (800) 444-7275 or (415) 388-2070 for more information.

13. Frank's Valley Group Horse Camp is the newest camp in Mount Tamalpais State Park. Opened in 1990, it's located on the lower Muir Beach Road at Santos Meadow. Facilities include campsites accommodating groups with two to twelve horses, picnic tables, pit toilets, fire pits, and water. For reservations and permits, call (415) 388-2070.

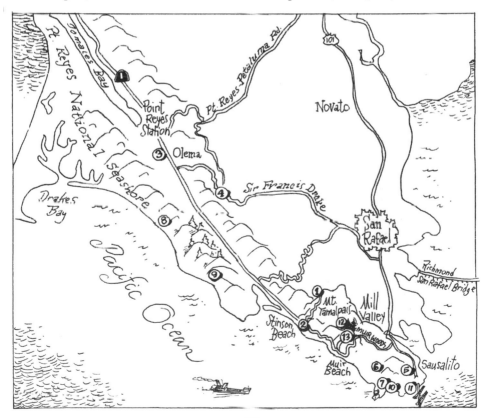

What are the best beaches in the area?

That depends on what you want to do—beach-combing, swimming, sunbathing, picnicking, or water sports. Let's start in the Marin Headlands at the north end of the Golden Gate Bridge and explore along the coast.

The Marin Headlands cover 12,000 acres stretching from Point Bonita at the south end to Muir Beach in the north. The coast here has several beaches that are not recommended for swimming because of rough surf and riptides (undertow), but they do offer beachcombing and hiking possibilities. Rodeo Beach and its quiet lagoon offer easy access, great beachcombing, picnicking spots, hiking trails, birding, and wave watching. At the north end of the beach is an area that's popular with local surfers. A pleasant 0.6-mile walk through Tennessee Valley in Mill Valley brings you to Tennessee Valley Beach, a scenic but narrow beach wedged between two high cliffs. The surf here is generally rough, but the beach is popular with hikers who want to explore the many trails in the headlands. Although Muir Beach has dangerous offshore waters and no lifeguard, it does combine a dramatic ocean break and a small, beautiful lagoon with calm waters for splashing and swimming at your own risk. There's also a wonderful picnic area complete with tables, toilets, grills, and fire rings. At the north end of Muir Beach is a clothing-optional area called Red Rock Beach.

Swimmers and surfers head for Stinson Beach State Park, a favorite ocean recreation area since the turn of the century. The beach is a 3-mile-long sandbar with no rocks, lots of white sand, and lifeguards on duty May through October. You can even borrow a volleyball net and ball from the lifeguards in exchange for a driver's license. Although the average summer water temperature is 58 degrees, that doesn't stop legions of beach and water enthusiasts from filling the parking lots and picnic areas by 11 a.m. on hot days in the summer and early fall. I'd suggest you call the ranger station at (415) 868-0942, or the surf and parking hotline at (415) 868-1922, to check on conditions before making the arduous drive over Mount Tamalpais. The park is open from 8 a.m. to 6 p.m. daily, and there's no day-use fee.

In the northern part of the GGNRA lies Tomales Bay State Park, which offers areas for picnicking and swimming on both sides of the bay and restricted camping on the west side. If you drive 8 miles north of Point Reyes Station on Highway 1, you'll reach Millerton Point and Alan P. Sieroty Beach, which offer equipped picnic spots and beach access. On the other side of Tomales Bay, try Heart's Desire Beach for picnics, swimming, and overnight camping (for hikers and bikers only). The park is open from 8 a.m. to 6 p.m., and the day-use fee is $5 per vehicle (no overnight parking allowed). Call the ranger station at (415) 669-1140 for more information.

Point Reyes National Seashore lies at the northernmost point of the GGNRA. It hosts every kind of shoreline area, from the wild, windswept beaches in the northwest to the more protected Drakes Beach and Limantour Beach to the south. Although most of the areas are too cold and rugged for swimming, they provide some great beachcombing, hiking, and backcountry camping. Call the Bear Valley Visitor Center at (415) 663-1092 for more information. For backcountry camping reservations, call (415) 663-8054 (9 a.m.– 2 p.m. weekdays).

NATIONAL MONUMENT OR NATIONAL PARK?

Within the National Park System of the Department of the Interior, 378 areas now have official status as important national assets. Of these, 54 are national parks and 73 are national monuments. Others are battlefields, historic sites, lakeshores, memorials, military parks, parkways, preserves, recreation areas, rivers and river-ways, scenic trails, and seashores. The nation's capital contains several designated sites, including the White House and the National Capital Park.

Regardless of their designation, the mission of these places is the same—to preserve and protect their resources for the enjoyment of the American public. National parks, such as Yosemite, Yellowstone, and Grand Canyon, are always established by an act of Congress, while national monuments, such as Muir Woods, can be established by presidential proclamation. But Congress also has the right to name monuments, as it did for George Washington's Birthplace in Virginia, Canyon de Chelly in Arizona, Pipestone in Minnesota, and Congaree Swamp in South Carolina.

National monuments are generally smaller in area than national parks and have less diversity or fewer attractions, but they are just as valuable as public resources. Because the 73 national monuments vary in character, the designation tells little about the nature, size, and management of the area, or how visitors experience the site. Here's a list of our national monuments as of March 1999:

Agate Fossil Beds, Nebraska
Allbates Flint Quarries, Texas
Aniakchak, Alaska
Aztec Ruins, New Mexico
Bandelier, New Mexico
Black Canyon of the Gunnison, Colorado
Booker T. Washington, Virginia
Buck Island Reef, Virgin Islands
Cabrillo, California
Canyon de Chelly, Arizona
Cape Krusenstern, Alaska
Capulin Volcano, New Mexico
Casa Grande, Arizona
Castillo de San Marcos, Florida
Castle Clinton, New York
Cedar Breaks, Utah
Chiricahua, Arizona
Colorado, Colorado
Congaree Swamp, South Carolina
Craters of the Moon, Idaho
Devils Postpile, California
Devils Tower, Wyoming
Dinosaur, Colorado-Utah
Effigy Mounds, Iowa
El Malpais, New Mexico
El Morro, New Mexico
Florissant Fossil Beds, Colorado
Fort Frederica, Georgia
Fort Matanzas, Florida
Fort McHenry, Maryland
Fort Pulaski, Georgia
Fort Stanwix, New York
Fort Sumter, South Carolina
Fort Union, New Mexico
Fossil Butte, Wyoming
George Washington Birthplace, Virginia
George Washington Carver, Missouri

Gila Cliff Dwellings, New Mexico
Grand Portage, Minnesota
Great Sand Dunes, Colorado
Hagerman Fossil Beds, Idaho
Hohokam Pima, Arizona
Homestead, Nebraska
Hovenweep, Colorado-Utah
Jewel Cave, South Dakota
John Day Fossil Beds, Oregon
Lava Beds, California
Little Bighorn Battlefield, Montana
Montezuma Castle, Arizona
Muir Woods, California
Natural Bridges, Utah
Navajo, Arizona
Ocmulgee, Georgia
Oregon Caves, Oregon
Organ Pipe Cactus, Arizona
Petroglyph, New Mexico
Pinnacles, California
Pipe Spring, Arizona
Pipestone, Minnesota
Poverty Point, Louisiana
Rainbow Bridge, Utah
Russell Cave, Alabama
Salinas Pueblo Missions, New Mexico
Scotts Bluff, Nebraska
Statue of Liberty, New York-New Jersey
Sunset Crater Volcano, Arizona
Timpanogos Cave, Utah
Tonto, Arizona
Tuzigoot, Arizona
Walnut Canyon, Arizona
White Sands, New Mexico
Wupatki, Arizona
Yucca House, Colorado

IV
Lodging and Dining

Where can we stay or camp overnight near Muir Woods?

No matter which direction you take from Muir Woods, you'll find some of the Bay Area's most charming places to spend the night, within a 10-mile radius (see the map on page 88). In addition to inns, cottages, and hotels, the area boasts two hostels for economical overnights. For information about inns in the Point Reyes National Seashore area, call (415) 663-1420.

MOUNT TAMALPAIS (3 MILES FROM ENTRANCE)

Mountain Home Inn	10 rooms
810 Panoramic Highway	$139–$259
Mill Valley	Includes breakfast
(415) 381-9000	

A bit of heaven on the side of Mount Tam. It's a close walk to Muir Woods from this charming hillside retreat overlooking San Francisco Bay. Some rooms have fireplaces and Jacuzzi baths.

MUIR BEACH (2.5 MILES FROM ENTRANCE)

Pelican Inn	7 rooms
Muir Beach	$163–$185
(415) 383-6000	Includes full English breakfast

A cozy English inn, complete with a pub and a snug! Close to Muir Woods and Muir Beach, the Pelican Inn is a taste of sixteenth-century England's West Country. Private bathrooms.

STINSON BEACH (8 MILES FROM ENTRANCE)

Casa del Mar	6 rooms
37 Belvedere Avenue	$150–$260
Stinson Beach	Includes breakfast, evening hors
(415) 868-2124	d'oeuvres
(800) 552-2124	

A stunning garden setting in a lively beach town. Views of the ocean and Mount Tamalpais from an art-filled home. Private bathrooms.

| *Sandpiper Motel* | 9 rooms and cabins |
| #1 Marine Way | $90–$135 |

Stinson Beach
(415) 868-1632
A charming beachside location. All rooms have cable TVs, VCRs, gas
fireplaces, refrigerators. Some kitchen units.

MILL VALLEY (DOWNTOWN IS 6 MILES FROM MUIR WOODS)

Mill Valley Inn
165 Throckmorton
Mill Valley
(415) 389-6608
(800) 595-2100

25 rooms and cottages
$155–$240
Includes continental breakfast
and parking

European charm nestled in California redwoods in the heart of Mill
Valley. Some rooms with fireplaces and private balconies.

Holiday Inn Express
160 Shoreline Highway
Mill Valley
(415) 332-5700

100 rooms
$105–$135

Convenient, clean, and reasonably priced; near the water. Heated
swimming pool. All rooms have cable TVs, and some have refrigerators.

SAUSALITO (8 MILES FROM MUIR WOODS)

The Inn above Tide
30 El Portal
Sausalito
(415) 332-9535
(800) 893-8433

30 rooms and suites
$195–$485
Includes continental breakfast
and sunset wine and cheese

If you were any closer to the water, you'd be on a boat! Beautiful
views of San Francisco and the bay. Most rooms have private decks
over the water and fireplaces.

The Gables Inn
62 Princess Street
Sausalito
(415) 289-1100
(800) 966-1554

9 rooms
$155–$300
Includes continental breakfast
and evening wine and cheese

This beautifully renovated three-story hotel, originally built in 1869,
was the first hotel to serve Sausalito. Some rooms offer fireplaces and
oversize tubs.

Alta Mira
125 Bulkley
Sausalito
(415) 332-1350

30 rooms and cottages
$80–$200

A landmark hillside hotel with sweeping views of San Francisco Bay
from balcony rooms, suites, and cottages.

Hotel Sausalito
16 El Portal
Sausalito
(415) 332-0700
(888) 442-0700

16 rooms
$125–$270
Includes morning coffee

Charming rooms showcase works by local artisans. Centrally located and near the water.

Casa Madrona Hotel
801 Bridgeway
Sausalito
(415) 332-0502
(800) 567-9524

35 rooms and cottages
$138–$260
Includes breakfast and evening social hour

A romantic getaway in the center of town. Every room is unique, with names such as Casa Cabana, Lord Ashley's Lookout, and Kathmandu. Overlooking San Francisco Bay, some rooms have fireplaces and tiled tubs.

HOSTELS
MARIN HEADLANDS
Golden Gate Hostel
Rodeo Valley
Marin Headlands
Sausalito
(415) 331-2777

103 beds, including dorms, family rooms, and private rooms
$12, dorm lodging
$35, family and private rooms

A three-story historic military home in a beautiful coastal valley within walking distance of Rodeo Lagoon and Beach, seacoast fortifications, and miles of trails in the Marin Headlands. You can rent sheets for $1 each and towels for 50 cents each or bring your own sleeping bag and linens. Kitchen facilities are provided; bring and cook your food.

POINT REYES NATIONAL SEASHORE
Point Reyes Hostel
Limantour Beach
Point Reyes National Seashore
(415) 663-8811 (7:30–9:30 a.m.; 4:30–9:30 p.m.)

45 beds in 4 dorms (2 in bunkhouse) and 1 family room
$12, adult; $6, child

A one-story ranch house right on the coast, with access to Limantour Beach and miles of hiking trails in the Point Reyes coastal wilderness. You can rent sheets and towels or bring your own. Full kitchen facilities are provided; bring and cook your own food.

The café, located just beyond the visitor center in Muir Woods, serves up quick breakfast and lunch items from 9 a.m. to 5 p.m. daily. It may not be a five-star restaurant, but its grub hits the spot after a walk in the woods. You can either eat inside, and look out into the woods through large picture windows, or enjoy the outdoors from picnic benches, where forest residents such as Steller's jays may try to talk you out of your leftovers. Remember never to feed the animals in Muir Woods. To stay healthy, they need food indigenous to the forest.

The café menu consists of breakfast muffins, Danish, and bagels for $1.75, ready-made sandwiches for $4–$5, hot dogs for $3.50, soup for $3.50, and a soup and salad combination for $5. Special kids' meals are available for $3.99. You can round out your lunch with chips, cookies, and a healthy selection of drinks. Coffee and espresso are available all day.

During nonpeak hours, many visitors use the café just as a comfortable and quiet place to read, write, sketch, or rendezvous with friends. The cafe's interior is light, with natural wood walls displaying historic photos of Muir Woods. The large windows give you the feeling that you're deep in the woods.

Where can we dine in the nearby towns?

There are lots of choice places to eat in the areas adjacent to Muir Woods. (Refer to the map on page 88.) For information on great eating at inns in the Point Reyes National Seashore area, call (415) 663-1420. In the listings that follow, $ means moderate prices, $$ higher than moderate.

MUIR BEACH (2.5 MILES FROM ENTRANCE TO MUIR WOODS)
Pelican Inn
Muir Beach at Highway 1
(415) 383-6000
English country cooking at an inn and pub on the low road to Stinson Beach. Lunch, dinner; closed Mondays during the winter; credit cards; $.

MOUNT TAMALPAIS (3 MILES FROM ENTRANCE TO MUIR WOODS)
Mountain Home Inn
810 Panoramic Highway
Mill Valley
(415) 381-9000
New American cuisine on the high road to Muir Woods. Lunch, dinner, weekend brunch; credit cards; $.

STINSON BEACH (8 MILES FROM ENTRANCE TO MUIR WOODS)
Sand Dollar Restaurant
3458 Shoreline Highway
Stinson Beach
(415) 868-0434
Seafood, pasta, and steak, in cozy beach cottage. Lunch, dinner, Sunday brunch; full bar; credit cards; $.

Stinson Beach Bar and Grill
3465 Shoreline Highway
Stinson Beach
(415) 868-2002
Barbecued oysters, Southwestern specialties, seafood, pasta, and grilled items. Lunch, dinner; outdoor dining; full bar; credit cards; $.

Parkside
43 Arenal Avenue
Stinson Beach
(415) 868-1272
Breakfast is a big event here, with specials all day. Breakfast, lunch,

dinner; snack bar (my personal favorite) open during good beach
weather; credit cards; $$.

MILL VALLEY (DOWNTOWN IS 6 MILES FROM MUIR WOODS)
Buckeye Roadhouse
15 Shoreline
Mill Valley
(415) 331-2600
Great comfort food, and plenty of it! Lunch, dinner, Sunday brunch; full
bar; credit cards; $$.

Cantina
651 East Blithedale
Mill Valley
(415) 381-1070
Spicy Mexican specials plus great margaritas. Lunch, dinner; full bar;
credit cards; $.

Dipsea Café
200 Shoreline Highway
Mill Valley
(415) 381-0298
Delicious country breakfasts, signature pancakes, on the road to Muir
Woods. Breakfast, lunch; credit cards; $$.

Frantoio's
152 Shoreline Highway
Mill Valley
(415) 289-5777
Cool Italian decor and a working olive press in harvest season. Lunch,
dinner; full bar; credit cards; $$.

Piazza d'Angelo
22 Miller Avenue
Mill Valley
(415) 388-2000
In the heart of Mill Valley's charming town center, delicious Italian spe-
cialties. Lunch, dinner; full bar; credit cards; $$.

SAUSALITO (8 MILES FROM MUIR WOODS)
Cat 'n' Fiddle
303 Johnson
Sausalito
(415) 332-4912
Daily California cuisine specials and spectacular views of Sausalito har-
bor. Lunch, dinner; full bar; credit cards; $$.

Charthouse
201 Bridgeway
Sausalito
(415) 332-0804
Seafood and steak in a wonderful
historic waterfront location.
Dinner; full bar; credit cards; $$.

Fred's Coffee Shop
1917 Bridgeway
Sausalito
(415) 332-4575
Cash only for a rich, big breakfast
served family style. Breakfast,
lunch; $.

Gatsby's
39 Caledonia Street
Sausalito
(415) 332-4500
A sampling of California cuisine and thick, juicy pizzas. Lunch, dinner;
full bar; credit cards; $.

Tommy's Wok
3001 Bridgeway
Sausalito
(415)332-5818
Heart-healthy Chinese food—delicious! Lunch, dinner; credit cards; $.

Spinnaker Restaurant
100 Spinnaker Drive
Sausalito
(415) 332-1500
Seafood specialties at a spot on the water with a view of San Francisco.
Lunch, dinner; full bar; credit cards; $$.

Seven Seas
682 Bridgeway
Sausalito
(415) 332-1304
Large portions of seafood. Casual, covered-patio dining. Lunch, dinner;
full bar; credit cards; $–$$.

Feng Nian
2650 Bridgeway
Sausalito
(415) 331-5300
A wide selection of Szechwan, Mandarin, and Hunan dishes. Lunch,
dinner; credit cards; $.

Where are the best picnic spots?

Although you can't picnic in Muir Woods, the surrounding parklands and open spaces have some of Northern California's best places to bring your basket, blanket, and bottle of wine. Let's start our picnic-hunting expedition in the Marin Headlands, at the north end of the Golden Gate Bridge.

MARIN HEADLANDS

The grassy parade ground and surrounding coastal hills of East Fort Baker provide great picnic spots, with spectacular views of the San Francisco skyline and protection from the wind and fog. East Road has some easily accessed tables as it climbs up the hill toward Sausalito, and if you drive out toward the ocean you'll find well-equipped spots along Rodeo Lagoon. For a view of the beach, drive a little farther to the Rodeo Beach parking area, offering tables, grills, water, and restrooms accessible by disabled people. In Tennessee Valley, you can search for an appealing spot by following one of the side paths into the valley's secluded areas or trek all the way to the beach at Tennessee Cove for a picture-perfect oceanside picnic. Pick up supplies in Sausalito. For information on any of these areas, call the Marin Headlands Visitor Center at (415) 331-1540.

MOUNT TAMALPAIS

There are two designated picnic areas on Mount Tam. Bootjack Picnic Area is in a wooded spot off Panoramic Highway just east of the Pan Toll Ranger Station. It's equipped with barbecues, tables, restrooms, and running water. East Peak Picnic Area is at the end of East Ridgecrest Boulevard. It has the same facilities as Bootjack, except for barbecues (no fires are allowed at East Peak). That still leaves plenty of spectacular country around Mount Tam for you to create your own custom site. Two of my favorite spots are Mountain Theater and the knolls along the Bolinas-Fairfax Road. Pick up supplies in either Sausalito or Mill Valley. For more information, call the Pan Toll Ranger Station at (415) 388-2070.

MUIR BEACH AND OVERLOOK

One of the best small beach picnic areas is at Muir Beach, where you'll find picnic tables, barbecue grills, restrooms, and a changing area in a sheltered

spot next to Muir Beach lagoon.
If you're looking for dramatic views and
aren't afraid of a
stiff ocean breeze, try the picnic area
high atop Muir Beach Overlook. Just be
prepared to batten down the paper cups. For more
information, call the Muir Woods Ranger Station at (415) 388-2596.

STINSON BEACH

For a picnic spiced with a little surf and sand, Stinson Beach offers a
large area, with tables, barbecues, and restrooms. There's a snack bar
near the main lifeguard tower, or you can pick up supplies at
Beckers-by-the-Bay grocery in the town of Stinson Beach. For more
information, call the Stinson Beach Ranger Station at (415) 868-0942.

OLEMA VALLEY

East of the Olema Valley on Sir Francis Drake Boulevard is Samuel P.
Taylor State Park, in a shady redwood forest with the soothing sounds
of a creek. The picnic area has tables, barbecues, water, and flush toilets. For information, call (415) 488-9897. If
you're heading north on West Ridgecrest
Boulevard from Mount Tam, just before the
Bolinas-Fairfax Road you'll see an old
apple orchard that provides sheltered picnic spots. Driving north on Highway 1,
between Bolinas Lagoon and Olema,
you'll probably see cars parked along-
side the road at an informal parking
area that marks the path to Hagmaeir
Pond, a small farm pond popular with
sunbathers and picnickers. Don't be shocked if some of the swimmers
follow the clothing-optional policy. For more information, call the
Bear Valley Visitor Center at (415) 663-1092.

TOMALES BAY AND POINT REYES NATIONAL SEASHORE

Tomales Bay State Park provides some great picnic spots on both
sides of the bay. Try Millerton Point and Alan P. Sieroty Beach on the
northwest side, or Heart's Desire Beach on the southwest side. Call
(415) 669-1140 for more information. Point Reyes National Seashore
offers unlimited picnicking possibilities. You can start at the Bear
Valley Visitor Center Picnic Area, or call (415) 663-1092 for more
information.

Can we hike to any restaurants and inns in the area?

Preferably with a shower!

Definitely. Some of the area's best inns and eating places are within hiking distance of Muir Woods. More adventuresome hikers can plan a several-day trek from inn to inn along spectacular trails on the Pacific Coast. Mountain Home Inn and Pelican Inn cater to overnight guests, while others—the Tourist Club, Green Gulch Guest House, and West Point Inn—allow overnight guests in restricted situations. The inns of Point Reyes National Seashore offer a wide variety of charming bed-and-breakfast lodgings. See the map on page 92 to locate inns and roads.

Mountain Home Inn and Pelican Inn are great starting or ending points for multi-day hikes with overnight stays; they're also perfect destinations for day hikes or places to rest and get a bit of refreshment in the middle of a hike. For telephone numbers and more information about these inns, see page 82. Be sure to call ahead for reservations and hours.

The Tourist Club is a great stopover spot for long hikes (see pages 69–70). This historic hiking clubhouse along Ocean View Trail has a lovely deck, picnic tables, and washrooms, and you can also refresh yourself with beer, wine, and soft drinks there. Only members can stay overnight. The club hosts an annual Octoberfest complete with a polka band and all the trimmings, steins of beer, and hearty plates of traditional German food—not to be missed. Call (415) 388-9987 for more information.

West Point Inn is at the end of a 2-mile hike from Pan Toll. It's the only historic structure that has survived from the days of the Mount Tamalpais and Muir Woods Railroad. The inn offers wonderful views and picnic tables; Tuesdays through Sundays lemonade, granola bars, and coffee are served. If you want something more, bring it with you. Overnight lodging in rustic rooms or cabins (without electricity) is for members of the West Point Inn Association. For membership information, call (415) 388-9955.

You can reach Green Gulch Guest House by the Coastal Trail and other trails. Its twelve quiet rooms are in a unique octagon structure made with traditional Japanese building techniques. This small retreat is within a Zen Buddhist community—the Green Gulch Farm Zen Center—that includes a meditation center, organic farm, and conference center. Overnight lodging is limited, but if you get a place you'll be treated to vegetarian meals as well. Call (415) 383-3134 for more information.

With so many inns and visitors in the Point Reyes area, I'd advise you to call the main referral service at (415) 663-1420 for information and reservations well in advance of your arrival.

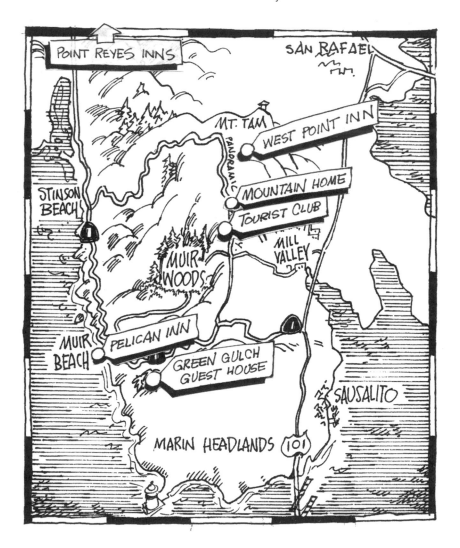

Any special seasonal events in Muir Woods?

Life in a redwood forest is so dependent on the changing seasons, it's only fitting that we celebrate with winter and summer solstice events. We also celebrate Muir Woods's Earth Day with January habitat restoration activities in the woods. These events are normally attended not by large crowds but rather by local residents and visitors who have a special attachment to the woods and want to share their appreciation of this place with family, friends, and park staff.

In June, at the summer solstice, we prepare a day-long program of events and activities to entertain, inform, and educate the public about the many aspects of forest life. Many of our festivities take place in the first parking lot, with walks and hikes leading into the woods. The day ends with a bonfire at the continent's edge, Muir Beach.

As the days grow shorter in December, we celebrate the beginning of the wet and wild season at the winter solstice. The event begins in the early evening and lasts for several hours, ending with a magical walk through the woods on paths lit by *luminaria* candles. There's hot cider to ease the chill, and plenty of singing to celebrate this special season.

We have our own version of Earth Day in January, the best month for habitat restoration and planting. Our program of activities related to restoring the natural environment includes interpretive walks through successfully restored habitat areas and replanting or working on areas that need extra attention. We supply snacks and drinks to the volunteers on this enjoyable and productive day.

For more information on these events, contact the Muir Woods Ranger Office at (415) 388-2596.

The Migration

Every fall, monarch butterflies throughout North America migrate to sites in California or central Mexico in search of milder climates. This spectacular migration is unique among insects: the North American monarch is the only insect in the world known to make the kind of annual, long-distance migration that birds and whales make. The monarchs fly west and south to the same sites each year—and frequently to the same trees. In spring they depart, flying north and east in search of milkweed plants, on which the females lay as many as 400 eggs. The adult butterflies die soon after, leaving their young to become the next generation of spring butterflies.

Monarch Winter Habitats

In California, monarchs cluster from about October to February in three kinds of habitats that play an important role in their migration. Overwintering habitats are usually found in coastal groves of eucalyptus or Monterey pine, often in a canyon or drainage that provides water. This microclimate offers stable day and night temperatures, protection from sunlight and wind, and ample moisture. Autumnal roost sites generally host smaller populations of monarchs for a few weeks or a couple of months in the fall and early winter. They may serve as feeding grounds, where monarchs replenish their fat reserves before winter sets in. Nectaring bivouac sites have a consistent flow of monarchs; these are the places where the butterflies nectar; then they return to their clusters elsewhere.

Do Monarchs Cluster in Muir Woods?

No, but you can see monarchs overwintering at nearby Muir Beach at a site that has been protected through the efforts of a local educator, Elizabeth Terwilliger. Autumnal roosts are found throughout the Muir Beach area and at Green Gulch Farm Zen Center. And you might see monarchs nectaring in sunny spots in Muir Woods.

The Future of the Migration

Scientists believe that, unless overwintering habitats in Mexico and California are protected, the monarch migration could soon disappear. It will take large, collaborative efforts among landowners, developers, and local governments to preserve this world-famous butterfly in its migration to Mexico and along California's coastal forests.

(Adapted from excerpts of *The Monarch Habitat Handbook* by Lincoln P. Brower, Mia Monroe, and Katrin Snow [Portland, OR: Xerxes Society, 1997].)

The Future of Muir Woods

Just as the natural ecology of Muir Woods continues to evolve, so does the administration of this national monument. As this handbook was being written, the National Park Service was undertaking a major long-term effort to solve critical issues, such as parking, traffic congestion, and the need to balance conservation of natural resources with the need to serve a growing number of visitors.

By the year 2004–2005, you might begin to see the results of this public planning effort—improved exhibits, more ecology-friendly pathways and boardwalks, greater focus on historic resources, better public access, and possibly an off-site parking and staging area with a shuttle service. Muir Woods is working regionally with other federal, state, and county agencies to better serve the needs of a growing population and a fragile ecosystem of ancient redwood trees, native plants, and endangered wildlife, in a small watershed where every drop of water is precious.

Muir Woods has joined a "watershed council" made up of representatives from the GGNRA, California Department of Fish and Game, Mount Tamalpais State Park, various county agencies, and the neighboring communities of Muir Beach and Green Gulch Farm Zen Center. The council's goal is to preserve natural resources while avoiding negative impacts on the communities that surround the region's urban parklands. To succeed, the council must establish working relationships with local communities and involve residents and community leaders. Unless we seek and plan solutions that involve the people who will use and share these resources, all of us risk losing the very treasures we're trying to preserve.

Ranger Farewell

I hope that I've answered all of your questions about Muir Woods and that you've learned some inside information on ways to make your visit to the woods more enjoyable.

The next section in the book, called Quick Reference, is filled with easy-to-find facts, forms, and information about the woods. The subjects are in alphabetical order so you can find what you need quickly without having to thumb through the whole handbook. My favorite is a trivia section that answers questions I may not have covered in the rest of the book.

Good hunting, and be sure to let us know if we need to change anything to improve future versions of this book. You can write to me, or to Susan and Phil Frank, c/o Pomegranate, Box 6099, Rohnert Park, CA 94927.

Bye for now,

Ranger Mia

Quick Reference

CLOTHES
Sturdy hiking boots
Thick hiking socks
Jeans, fleece pants, and sweatshirt
Rain-resistant jacket, poncho, and pants
Warm hat and gloves
Extra clothes for layering: T-shirt, long-sleeved flannel shirt, down vest or light jacket
Large bandanna
UV-protection sunglasses

EQUIPMENT
Rain-resistant sleeping bag and pad
Backpacking tent and stakes
Frame backpack (for long hikes and overnight trips)
Flashlight or headlamp, extra alkaline batteries, and spare bulb
Water bottle (at least quart-size)
Backpacking stove and fuel
Cooking pot, cup, and utensils
Fire starter kit (waterproof matches in waterproof container, candle, and dry paper)
Topographical map and compass
Pocket knife
Watch
Water purification device

SUPPLIES
Sunscreen
Insect repellent
Lip balm
Small first-aid kit with blister care items
Toilet items
Food (including emergency rations such as raisins, nuts, hard candies)
Extra zip-lock bags

1838 Grant of 19,000 acres of southern Marin county, including the area that is now Muir Woods National Monument, was made by the Mexican government to William Antonio Richardson. The land was known as Rancho Sausalito.

1840 Logging of Marin's timber began early in the decade, and within 30 years most of the old-growth redwood was harvested. The redwood canyon was spared the ax and saw because of its inaccessibility and the fact that it drained to the ocean rather than the bay, making transport of the logs nearly impossible.

1886 The first structure in the canyon, the Ben Johnson Cabin, was constructed of alder and leased by the Tamalpais Sportsmen's Club for deer-hunting purposes. Johnson, who occupied the cabin until after the turn of the century, served as "keeper" for the property. According to period reports, he befriended skunks and deer, which fed from his hand.

1890 William Kent first heard of the stand of old-growth coast redwoods and was encouraged by a friend to purchase the land from the Tamalpais Land and Water Company.

1892 In September, the Bohemian Club of San Francisco, an organization of writers, artists, musicians, and civic leaders, rented a portion of the redwood canyon for its annual Summer Encampment, during which club members put on a play and skits based on a theme. The 1892 theme required a 40-foot-tall statue of a seated Buddha, which sculptor F. Marion Wells constructed of lath and plaster. The Bohemians camped for one night, but found the location too cold; they eventually purchased a permanent home on the Russian River. The mammoth Buddha was torn down soon after.

1896 The Mill Valley and Mount Tamalpais Scenic Railway was incorporated, and construction of a railbed to the top of the mountain began in February. Its construction eventually resulted in easy access to the redwood valley.

1905 William Kent purchased the 611 acres of land known as Sequoia Canyon for $45,000. Kent, a stockholder in the scenic railway, then sold a large tract of the land to the company for the extension of a branch line of the railroad into the canyon.

1905 The first Dipsea Race, an annual footrace over the mountain that continues to this day, was run from Mill Valley to Stinson Beach (known at the turn of the century as Willow Camp). The 7-mile course of the race crossed through what is now Muir Woods.

1906 A great earthquake and fire devastated San Francisco. Efforts were begun to acquire Sequoia Canyon, by condemnation, if necessary, for its lumber and its potential as a reservoir, both much needed to help rebuild San Francisco.

1907 The first train entered Kent's Sequoia Canyon on the branch line of the Mill Valley and Mount Tamalpais Scenic Railway.

1907 William Kent corresponded directly with President Theodore Roosevelt about his desire and intention to donate the canyon and its stand of old-growth redwood trees to the national government to be preserved as a park. U.S. Chief Forester Gifford Pinchot supported Kent's plan. Roosevelt responded positively, but felt the area should be named in honor of Kent himself instead of Kent's choice, naturalist John Muir.

1908 On January 9, President Roosevelt declared Muir Woods a national monument—the seventh national monument and the first created from lands donated by a private individual.

1908 The first automobile, a Winton, was driven into Muir Woods over the old wagon road from Mill Valley.

1909 John Muir visited Muir Woods, Ben Johnson's cabin, and the newly constructed Muir Inn, where he was photographed with William Kent. Muir and Kent became close friends, and Muir visited the Kent family in Kentwood and explored the woods on several occasions with Kent.

John Muir and William Kent

1910 A plaque honoring Gifford Pinchot, first head of the Forest Service, was established by a group of Sierra Club members.

1910 William Kent was elected to Congress as a progressive Roosevelt–Johnson Republican. He served as a representative for seven years.

1910 Six years after the National Park Service was created, the federal government appointed the first "custodian" for the monument, Andrew Lind, allotting $900 per annum as a wage. Park rangers were not officially assigned to Muir Woods until 1921.

1913 On June 12, the Muir Inn burned to the ground; a faulty flue on a wood burning stove was suspected as the cause. On July 7, less than four weeks later, a week-long fire scorched Mount Tamalpais, consuming 2,000 acres, including ten visitor cabins next to the site of the burned inn. Fought by 3,000 men, the fire was eventually extinguished at the site of the former inn.

1914 John Muir died on Christmas Eve.

1921 Richard F. O'Rourke was appointed ranger-in-charge of Muir Woods. He served as a National Park Service superintendent.

1923 Automobiles were officially banned inside Muir Woods. The main trail that visitors follow today had been a through auto road to the Muir Inn before this, and parking was allowed around the redwood trees in designated spots.

1926 A toll road was completed and opened that allowed autos to visit the monument on a smooth (but unpaved) roadway. The toll exacted was 50 cents per auto and 15 cents per passenger.

William Kent

1927 The California state park system was initiated, and Mount Tamalpais State Park was created.

1928 William Kent died at his Kentfield home on March 13. In December, a rock was laid at the Kent Tree honoring him.

1929 The great Mill Valley fire burned 100 homes and stopped just short of Muir Woods when the winds shifted. The railroad discontinued Muir Woods branch operations immediately after the fire. Within a year the railroad had closed down, a victim of the automobile.

1931 A ranger spotted a mountain lion, the first of several reliable sightings during the 1930s. The big cats, while elusive and seldom seen, still roam Mount Tamalpais.

1932 On April 7, the *San Francisco Examiner* ran a "Ripley's Believe It or Not" column claiming that "the upside-down redwood" in Muir Woods was alive and well. The inaccurate item spurred a flood of inquiries that caused the head ranger to seek a retraction of the item.

1932 An epidemic caused the disappearance of the gray squirrel from Muir Woods. In the years to come only occasional sightings were reported.

Curio Shop

1933 The first curio shop was built at Muir Woods.

1933 In October, a Civilian Conservation Corps camp was established at the former site of the Muir Woods Inn. The CCC was created by President Franklin D. Roosevelt as a work program during the depression to provide work for unemployed craft workers. The goal of the corps was to upgrade and enhance public park lands. Crews worked extensively throughout Muir Woods, building bridges, fire trails, creek riprap, and staff housing. The CCC workers quarried local rock for construction of the Fern Creek Bridge and the Mountain Theater. They built in a rustic style of construction commonly known as "parkitecture."

1937 The Golden Gate Bridge opened, making automobile access to Marin County and Muir Woods much easier.

1939 An abandoned tollhouse was being used by sixty-three-year-old soothsayer Lee Von Voss to sell fortunes. He was arrested and put on the first train out of town for soothsaying without authorization. His last prediction, according to published reports, was that a forthcoming "miracle" would destroy the tollhouse. That night it burned to the ground.

1945 United Nations representatives gathered in Muir Woods for a memorial to the late President Franklin D. Roosevelt and unveiled a commemorative plaque on a redwood log in Cathedral Grove. The ceremony was attended by more than a thousand people.

1954 Ranger reports noted a gray squirrel comeback and sightings of blue herons feeding on crayfish in the creek.

1968 Split-rail fences were built, to define trails and protect the redwoods' shallow roots from trampling.

1969 In September, internationally recognized sculptor Benny Bufano arrived in Muir Woods to install a statue that he had created in honor of peace. The National Park Service, seeking to keep the woods as natural as possible, allowed Bufano to display the statue in Cathedral Grove for one month.

1972 The Golden Gate National Recreation Area was established, encompassing numerous military facilities, state beaches, and local landmarks, including Muir Woods National Monument. The new park stretched along 28 miles of coastline in three California counties.

1989 The visitor center was built. Access for large buses over the twisting roads to Muir Woods was restricted.

1996 A prescribed burning program was initiated within the Muir Woods National Monument to restore the natural role of fire and prevent major unplanned wildfires.

1997 For the first time, a fee ($2 per adult) was charged for entrance to Muir Woods.

1999 The first redwood boardwalk was built to replace 470 feet of asphalt path. Hailed as a more environmentally friendly walkway through the woods, it put pedestrians above sensitive ground and plants that surround the redwoods.

(Partially excerpted from an unpublished manuscript by Wes Hildreth.)

The National Park Service offers programs tailored for elementary schoolchildren and teachers, suitable for a wide range of teaching styles and methods. Groups such as photography clubs, botany classes, native plant societies, and scouts who want to use the woods as a setting for their own learning experiences can arrange for ranger-led walks. For more information on education programs and fee waivers at Muir Woods, call (415) 388-2596.

TEACHER-DRIVEN, CURRICULUM-BASED PROGRAMS

If you're a teacher who wants to bring your class to Muir Woods, the National Park Service provides a variety of teacher resource materials for classroom learning before the students even get on the bus. A video, "Into the Forest," and activity guides give students a tour of the woods and lively exercises to help them learn about the area's ecology. Once the students arrive, a ranger gives an introduction and provides each student with a Discovery Kit for a self-guided, teacher-driven walk through the woods. Although the resource materials have been geared for third-grade classrooms, this program works well for all grades and ages.

For third-grade teachers who want to incorporate the subject of redwood forest ecology fully into their curriculum plan, the National Park Service offers a one-year program with a half-day visit to Muir Woods. This program begins with a teacher workshop that explores stream, forest, and edge habitats through the scientific method and art projects. Teachers return to their classrooms armed with a variety of class activities and teaching materials. This is followed by a ranger visit to the classroom in preparation for the field visit. The culmination of the program is a half-day visit to Muir Woods, where students are taken on a ranger-led but student-guided exploration of the forest with the help of a Discovery Kit and other materials. Every two years, the teachers return to Muir Woods for a half-day workshop to share results and start planning for next year. This kind of program requires a larger commitment from teachers, but the benefits for both students and teachers are that much greater.

SCHOOL TRANSPORTATION
Through donations received at a receptacle near the visitor center in Muir Woods, the National Park Service is able to provide bus transportation to Muir Woods for classes that otherwise wouldn't be able to come. Arrangements must be made well in advance of the visit by calling (415) 388-2596.

OTHER EDUCATION PROGRAMS
For public education programs in Mount Tamalpais State Park, including a series of lectures on astronomy and space-related sciences, from April to October in the Mountain Theater, contact (415) 388-2070 or (415) 455-5370.

GOLDEN GATE
NATIONAL
PARKS
ASSOCIATION

IF YOU ENJOY THE PARKS—JOIN US!

More than ever before, the Parks need the support of people like you. By joining the Association—the parks' non-profit partner—you'll be a part of our efforts to preserve the national parks at the Golden Gate.

As a member, you will help restore native habitats, maintain miles of trails, preserve historic landmarks and develop park education programs for young people.

JOIN THE PARKS ASSOCIATION AND YOU'LL RECEIVE:

- *Gateways*, a quarterly newsletter filled with park news and tips on special places
- *ParkEvents* calendar delivered to your home
- Invitations to members-only walks, talks and excursions
- Discounts at park bookstores
- Free use of the Alcatraz and Fort Point audio tours
- At $35 Park Partner level or above, two membership cards plus a special gift

---

Yes, I would like to join the Parks Association. Enclosed is my membership contribution of:

☐ **$25** Park Friend

☐ **$35** Park Partner (Includes the award-winning paperback *Guide to the Parks*)

☐ **$50** Park Sponsor (Includes a full-color Golden Gate National Parks totebag)

☐ **$100** Park Steward (Includes two ceramic Golden Gate National Parks mugs)

Donations are tax-deductible. For information on senior memberships, or to join by phone, call the Parks Association at (415) 561-3000.

Name _____

Address _____

City _____ State ____ Zip ____

Day Phone ( ) ____ Total amount enclosed $ ____

Make check or money order payable to Golden Gate National Parks Association

Charge to: ☐ Visa ☐ Mastercard

Signature _____

Account number _____ Expiration date ____

Please mail this coupon to:
Golden Gate National Parks Assoc., Fort Mason, Building 201, San Francisco, CA 94123

*If you love the Mountain
There's a place for you*

MT. TAMALPAIS
INTERPRETIVE
ASSOCIATION

P.O. Box 3318
San Rafael, CA 94912
(415) 258-2410

Membership: Sarah Davis
(415) 924-7887

The Mt. Tamalpais Interpretive Association is a volunteer organization whose purpose is to promote the conservation, education and interpretation of the State Park system, primarily at Mt. Tamalpais State Park. We do this in various ways which include:

- Volunteering at the Visitor Center on East Peak

- Sponsoring interpretive hikes for the public

- Sale or free distribution of interpretive and educational materials

- Aiding the State of California in conserving and interpreting the areas of the State Park system

- Fundraising to support these activities

Though the benefits of contributing to the Mt. Tamalpais Interpretive Association are endless, they include:

- Satisfaction in helping visitors learn about and preserve a beautiful resource

- Involvement with a group of wonderful people with similar goals and ideals

- Enriching activities such as weekly hikes and special educational walks

- Educational programs and training

- Discounts on most items we sell

- Voting privileges in the association

- A quarterly newsletter, The Mountain Log

Please join us. Just fill out the application below, include your check and mail both to the address above.

MT. TAMALPAIS INTERPRETIVE ASSOCIATION
Membership Application

Name _____   Day Phone _____

Address _____   Evening Phone _____

City _____   Zip Code _____

Special interest, knowledge or experience:
_____
_____
_____

Membership Fees (if you join between 1/1 & 9/30)
☐ $25.00 – Active Member - work 40 hrs per year
☐ $10.00 – Senior Active – same (over 65)
☐ $40.00 – Supporting Member
☐ $25.00 – Senior Supporting
☐ Donation

Alice Eastwood Trail: Named after famous botanist Alice Eastwood, who recognized the trail as a shortcut to the Potrero from West Point, this steep section on the Muir Woods–Alpine Lake route appeared on the earliest Marin Municipal Water District (MMWD) map.

Alpine Lake: Albert Reed Baker, an engineer with MMWD, named the lake for this area, which was known as Alpine, and he recommended building the dam that was completed here in 1919.

Ben Johnson's Cabin

Ben Johnson Cabin site: William Kent's caretaker and gamesman for the woods, Ben Johnson, lived in a cabin on this site and was visited here by many early notables, including John Muir and Gifford Pinchot.

Ben Johnson Trail: Even before the woods were named Muir Woods, while Ben Johnson was employed as William Kent's caretaker, he built this trail to connect with Lone Tree Trail.

Bohemian Grove: The Bohemian Club of San Francisco, an organization of writers, artists, musicians, and civic leaders, rented a portion of Muir Woods for its annual Summer Encampment in 1892. The club built a 40-foot-tall statue of a seated Buddha and placed it in a particular grove of trees, as a backdrop for a play and skits during the one-night encampment.

Bootjack Camp: When viewed from the Tourist Club, the grassy area above the present parking lot for this camp looked to some like a bootjack. The site was formerly called Camp Bohemia. The name Bootjack Trail first appeared on an 1898 hikers' map.

Camp Alice Eastwood: Not only a noted botanist and curator at the California Academy of Sciences, Alice Eastwood was also a prodigious hiker and author of numerous articles on the flora of Mount Tamalpais. The camp, used by the Civilian Conservation Corps during the depression, was dedicated in 1949 on Eastwood's ninetieth birthday. The lovely old Muir Inn (first of two, both gone now) once graced this site.

Cathedral Grove: Named for the circular formation of giant redwoods that allows sunlight to filter down, as in a cathedral.

Coastal Trail: In the 1970s, Bob Cook worked on a portion of this trail for his eagle scout badge. He was aided by Roy Winnie, the Young Adults, the Boy Scouts, the Sierra Club, and the Mill Valley Lions Club. The trail was officially opened in 1978.

Concrete Bridge: This popular fish-viewing location is near the boundary between Mount Tamalpais State Park and Muir Woods.

Conlon and Camino del Cañon (stub roads): Now incorporated in Muir Woods, these roads are remnants of an early effort to subdivide West Marin.

Dan Sealy's Pool: Named after a ranger who, while conducting a public program at the pool in 1980, unexpectedly decided to go for a swim. This popular fish-viewing spot is located beyond the second bridge.

Dias Ridge: Around 1919, ranch owner George Dias built a private road across the ridge of his property to connect the Sausalito–Bolinas Road (Highway 1) to the Muir Woods Road. Today this road serves as the southern extension of Panoramic Highway.

Dipsea Trail: Named after the Dipsea Inn at Stinson Beach, this route along the ridge west of Muir Woods was formerly miscalled the Lone Tree Trail (the tree in question is a redwood). The trail is now home to the famous Dipsea Race, an annual event that ends at the Pacific Ocean.

Druid Ridge: Often shrouded in fog at the edge of Muir Woods, this stand of eucalyptus shelters Marin's first hot tub.

East Peak: Frederick William Beechey, an early explorer and cartographer, was possibly the first Euro-American to climb this section of Mount Tamalpais in 1826. Blossom Rock in San Francisco Bay was named after his ship.

Eldridge Grade: John Oscar Eldridge, operator of the first gas plant in San Rafael, started collecting money to build this road in 1868. Construction began around 1884. Like many of Marin's roads, it was built with Chinese labor.

Cathedral Grove

Golden Gate Dairy: Currently a horse stable, this site once housed an early dairy farm.

Gravity Car Grade: This route was traveled by what was known as "the Crookedest Railroad in the World." A book of the same name, written by Ted Wurm and Al Graves, has photographs of passenger cars coasting into Muir Woods along this right-of-way.

Green Gulch Farm: This Zen retreat center and organic farm is located in a scenic forest setting. The gardens are open to the public.

Hawk Hill: The summit where Battery 129 was located has been renamed Hawk Hill because it is one of the nation's premier locations for observing birds of prey. Birders have counted nineteen species and claim to have seen 3,000 raptors in a single day.

Hidden Lake Trail: Formerly a portion of the Hidden Lake Fire Trail, which ran from Cataract Gulch to Bon Tempe Ranch. The lake is now a swamp called High Marsh.

Homestead Valley: This site, once occupied by a dairy ranch, now harbors a little-known trail that is ideal for dog walkers and hikers looking for spectacular bay vistas.

Kent Lake: This lake is named for Thomas T. Kent, a director of the MMWD from 1920 to 1959.

Kent Trail: First named Swede George Trail and later Kent Cabin Trail, the original route was affected greatly by the construction of Alpine Dam. The steps below Serpentine Point were constructed by the Sierra Club and other groups. The trail dates from at least 1898.

Laurel Dell: Named by John H. Cutter for its many bay (laurel) trees, this area was once known as Old Stove Trail, because an old iron stove, a remnant of a fire that destroyed a hunting cabin, sat by the trail for many years.

Lost Trail: This trail was constructed by members of the Tourist Club in 1914, only to be partially destroyed by a huge landslide in the mid-1930s. Ben Schmidt and friends set about rebuilding the route in the 1960s, and the project was completed in 1976 by California Youth Summer Program workers under the supervision of state park rangers.

Maple Meadow: This is the first open glade in the park, a favorite spot for ladybugs seeking horsetails in summer and fall.

Matt Davis Trail: Davis, who was known as the "Dean of Trail Workers," died in 1938, but his legacy remains. This extension from Pan Toll to Stinson Beach was built to offer a more level alternative to the Dipsea Trail. It was constructed in 1931 by Jonathon Webb and Dan Lear and later rerouted down Table Rock Creek by George Leonard, Ben Schmidt, and friends in the late 1960s.

Mountain Home Inn: Nothing remains of the original structure built here in 1912 by Oscar Meyer. The present building dates from 1985.

Muir Beach: This spot, where Redwood Creek meets the ocean, used to be called Big Lagoon.

Muir Woods: Named by William Kent (1864–1928), a local resident, early conservationist, and later congressman.

Old Inn: Once the site of a park concession, this location is now used as a conference center.

O'Rourke's Bench: Richard Festus O'Rourke, known affectionately as "Dad O'Rourke," was a builder and maintainer of trails, custodian of Muir Woods from May 1921 to June 1923, and president of the Mountain Play Association until 1935. The vista site for the bench is descriptively known as "Edge of the World," and the inscription reads: "Give me these hills and the friends I love. I ask no other heaven."

Panoramic Trail: This trail was constructed by Bob Murray, Frank Meraglia, Ben Schmidt, and volunteers in the 1960s.

Pan Toll: A tollhouse was located here near the Panoramic Highway on what was then called the Southside Toll Road, thus the name Pan Toll. The area was originally called Summit Meadow.

Rock Spring Trail: Named after Rock Spring, this trail has been in existence since the 1898 hikers' map, where it was called West Point Trail.

Santos Meadow: Now a horse pasture, the meadow is a remnant of past dairy operations.

Stapelveldt Trail: The trail is named after early San Franciscan William Stapelveldt, who built it. The Civilian Conservation Corps repaired it in 1939.

Steep Ravine Trail: Ebenezer Knowlton, known as the "hiking professor," (1835–1911), kept this route open. It was rebuilt by the CCC in 1936.

Stinson Beach: Site of the Dipsea Inn, this beach was the proposed terminus of an extension of the Mount Tamalpais Railway from West Point. The land was acquired in 1851 by Captain Alfred Darby Easkoot, who reputedly guarded his property with a shotgun and fired at anyone collecting driftwood. The beach was formerly known as Willow Camp.

Sun Trail: Originally called Cow Trail by Tourist Club members, this route was renamed Cove Trail because of a misreading by state park cartographers. W. E Jeffers christened the route Sun Trail on his 1945 map.

Tennessee Cove: A passenger ship called the *Tennessee* ran aground on the beach here in 1853 and left its name behind.

Tourist Club: The club was founded in 1912 by German-speaking immigrants as a branch of a European club (Touristen-Verein "Die Naturfreunde") founded in Vienna in 1878.

Van Wyck Meadow: Formerly called Lower Rattlesnake Camp, this popular picnicking area in the 1920s and 1930s was renamed for Sidney M. Van Wyck Jr., president of the Tamalpais Conservation Club in 1920–1921. A lawyer, he played an active role as an advocate for a state park.

West Peak: Originally called Table Hill, a name that remained into the 1880s, West Peak was once the highest (2,604 feet) of the three summits of Mount Tamalpais but lost the distinction when 24 feet were lopped off during the construction of an air force base atop it. The military has promised to one day give the property back to mountain lovers.

West Point Inn: Built in 1904 by the Mount Tamalpais Railway as the westernmost terminus of the line, West Point Inn was acquired by hiking groups in 1934, and for a time it was the headquarters of the Tamalpais Conservation Club. Today the inn is run by a nonprofit corporation.

Wobbly Rock: This big rock adjacent to Muir Beach received its name from beatniks in the 1950s.

The Golden Gate National Park Association (GGNPA) is a nonprofit organization dedicated to the preservation, improvement, and interpretation of lands within the GGNRA, including Muir Woods National Monument. For over a decade the GGNPA has worked hand-in-hand with the National Park Service to preserve and enhance parklands through its support of park service programs.

Ongoing efforts by the GGNPA and NPS resource managers at the GGNRA to preserve, protect, and restore native plants and wildlife of Muir Woods include the following programs:

- Propagating native plant species at the Muir Woods Nursery.

- Replanting native species and doing erosion-control work.

- Controlling the spread of non-native trees and plants.

- Counting and monitoring endangered or threatened wildlife species.

- Restoring native habitats, including:
  Understory of Muir Woods
  Redwood Creek habitat
  Songbird nesting habitats
  Muir Beach dunes
  Golden Gate Dairy
  Floodplains and wetlands in the lower Redwood Creek area

- Identifying, researching, and planning future preservation and restoration programs. A major restoration program has been identified for Big Lagoon at Muir Beach. The lagoon, an important transitional habitat for coho salmon and other aquatic life, has been depleted over time. The goal is to revitalize the lagoon in an effort to restore a diminishing wetlands habitat that is home to a variety of native bird and wildlife species.

For more information on these and other programs, contact the GGNPA at (415) 561-3000, or Carolyn Shoulders at the National Park Service Natural Resources Office (415) 331-0771, or Heather King at the Muir Woods Nursery (415) 388-3267. For a GGNPA membership application, see page 106.

CAMPING AND BACKPACKING
Campground Reservations
    Alice Eastwood Group Camp:
        Information . . . .(415) 388-2070
        Reservations . . . .(800) 444-7275
    Frank's Valley Group Horse Camp . . . .(415) 388-2070
Marin Headlands backpack camps:
    (Hawk, Haypress, Bicentennial) . . . .(415) 331-1540
Marin Headlands group camps:
    (Battery Alexander, Kirby Cove) . . . .(415) 561-4304
Olema Ranch Campground . . . .(415) 663-8001
Pan Toll Campground . . . .(415) 388-2070
Point Reyes National Seashore backpack camps (Glen, Wildcat, Coast):
    Information . . . .(415) 663-1092
    Reservations . . . .(415) 663-8054
Samuel P. Taylor State Park:
    Information . . . .(415) 488-9897
    Reservations . . . .(800) 444-7275
Steep Ravine Campground . . . .(800) 444-7275
National Park Service at Muir Woods . . . .(415) 388-2595
Prescribed burning in Muir Woods . . . .(415) 388-2596
Trail Conditions
    GGNRA . . . .(415) 556-0560
    Marin Headlands . . . .(415) 331-1540
    MMWD Lands . . . .(415) 459-5267
    Mount Tamalpais State Park . . . .(415) 388-2070

EDUCATIONAL PROGRAMS
Mount Tamalpais State Park
    education programs . . . .(415) 388-2070/455-5370
Muir Woods education programs . . . .(415) 388-2596
Muir Woods interpretive walks and talks . . . .(415) 388-2595

GETTING AROUND
Advance reservations for tours . . . .(415) 388-7368
Aramark Corporation
    (runs park café and gift shop) . . . .(415) 388-7059
Golden Gate National Parks Association . . . .(415) 388-7368
National Park Service at Muir Woods . . . .(415) 388-2595

GETTING THERE
Muir Woods school transportation . . . .(415) 388-2596

Tour and Transportation Companies to Muir Woods
Blue and Gold Ferry Tours . . . .(415) 705-5444
A Day in Nature Tours . . . .(415) 673-0548
Golden Gate Jeep Tours . . . .(415) 788-8687
Golden Gate Transit . . . .(415) 923-2000
Gray Line Tours . . . .(415) 558-9400
Tower Tours . . . .(415) 434-TOUR (8687)

LODGING AND DINING

Lodging

Mountain Home Inn . . . .(415) 381-9000
Pelican Inn, Muir Beach . . . .(415) 383-6000
Mill Valley
Holiday Inn Express . . . .(415) 332-5700
Mill Valley Inn . . . .(415) 389-6608/(800) 595-2100
Sausalito
Alta Mira . . . .(415) 332-1350
Casa Madrona Hotel . . . .(415) 332-0502/(800) 567-9524
The Gables Inn . . . .(415) 289-1100/(800) 966-1554
Hotel Sausalito . . . .(415) 332-0700/(888) 442-0700
The Inn above Tide . . . .(415) 332-9535/(800) 893-8433
Stinson Beach
Casa del Mar . . . .(415) 868-2124/(800) 552-2124
Sandpiper Motel . . . .(415) 868-1632

Hostels

Golden Gate Hostel . . . .(415) 331-2777
Point Reyes Hostel . . . .(415) 663-8811

Dining

Mountain Home Inn . . . .(415) 381-9000
Pelican Inn . . . .(415) 383-6000
Mill Valley
Buckeye Roadhouse . . . .(415) 331-2600
Cantina . . . .(415) 381-1070
Dipsea Café . . . .(415) 381-0298
Frantoio's . . . .(415) 289-5777
Piazza d'Angelo . . . .(415) 388-2000
Sausalito
Cat 'n' Fiddle . . . .(415) 332-4912
Charthouse . . . .(415) 332-0804
Feng Nian . . . .(415) 331-5300

Fred's Coffee Shop . . . .(415) 332-4575
Gatsby's . . . .(415) 332-4500
Seven Seas . . . .(415) 332-1304
Spinnaker Restaurant . . . .(415) 332-1500
Tommy's Wok . . . .(415) 332-5818
Stinson Beach
   Parkside . . . .(415) 868-1272
   Sand Dollar Restaurant . . . .(415) 868-0434
   Stinson Beach Bar and Grill . . . .(415) 868-2002

Hike-in Restaurants and Inns
(within hiking distance of Muir Woods)
Green Gulch Guest House . . . .(415) 383-3134
Inns of Point Reyes, information . . . .(415) 663-1420
Tourist Club . . . .(415) 388-9987
West Point Inn . . . .(415) 388-9955

Picnic Spots
Marin Headlands . . . .(415) 331-1540
Mount Tamalpais . . . .(415) 388-2070
Muir Beach and Overlook . . . .(415) 388-2596
Point Reyes National Seashore . . . .(415) 663-1092
Samuel P. Taylor State Park . . . .(415) 488-9897
Stinson Beach . . . .(415) 868-0942

PARK ATTRACTIONS
Audubon Canyon Ranch . . . .(415) 868-9244
Golden Gate Raptor Observatory . . . .(415) 331-0730
Hawkwatch Hotline . . . . (415) 561-3030, ext. 2500
Marin Headlands Visitor Center . . . .(415) 331-1540
Muir Woods interpretive walks and talks . . . .(415) 388-2595
Muir Woods Nursery . . . .(415) 388-3267
Point Reyes National Seashore
   Visitor Center . . . .(415) 663-1092
Salmon Spawning
   Redwood Creek, Muir Woods . . . .(415) 388-2596
   Lagunitas Creek (Samuel P. Taylor
      Park or Devil's Gulch) . . . .(415) 488-9897
   Lagunitas Creek (Shafter Bridge) . . . .(415) 459-5267
   Olema Creek, Five Brooks Trailhead . . . .(415) 663-1092

PRESERVATION AND VOLUNTEER PROGRAMS
GGNPA preservation programs in Muir Woods . . . . .(415) 561-3000
GGNPA volunteer programs in Muir Woods . . . . . .(415) 388-3267
GGNRA volunteer hotline . . . .(415) 561-4325
MMWD volunteer programs . . . .(415) 459-5267
Mount Tamalpais State Park volunteer programs
    Information . . . .(415) 258-2410
    Membership . . . .(415) 924-7887
Muir Woods Ranger Office . . . .(415) 388-2596
NPS Natural Resources Office . . . .(415) 331-0771
NPS Salmon Restoration Project . . . .(415) 868-0732

RECREATIONAL OPPORTUNITIES
Bear Valley Visitor Center . . . .(415) 663-1092
Five Brooks Ranch and Stables . . . .(415) 663-1570
Marin Headlands ranger-led walks and hikes . . . . . .(415) 331-1540
Mount Tamalpais Interpretive
    Association hikes . . . .(415) 258-2410/388-2070
Marin Bicycle Trails Council . . . .(415) 456-7512
Marin Municipal Water District fishing
    hotline . . . .(415) 459-0888
Miwok Livery Stables . . . .(415) 383-8048
Muir Woods ranger-led walks, talks, and hikes . . . . .(415) 388-2596
Point Reyes backcountry reservations . . . .(415) 663-8054
Point Reyes ranger-led walks and hikes . . . .(415) 663-1092
Stinson Beach Ranger Station . . . .(415) 868-0942
Stinson Beach surf and parking hotline . . . .(415) 868-1922
Tomales Bay State Park Ranger Station . . . .(415) 669-1140
Trail and road condition updates . . . .(415) 499-7191

SPECIAL SEASONAL EVENTS
Muir Woods's Earth Day (January) . . . .(415) 388-2596
Summer Solstice Celebration . . . .(415) 388-2596
Winter Solstice Celebration . . . .(415) 388-2596

SPECIAL SERVICES
Educational fee waivers . . . .(415) 388-2596
Muir Woods school transportation . . . .(415) 388-2596

GGNRA, SOUTH DISTRICT
Alcatraz information . . . .(415) 705-1042
Alcatraz boat transportation . . . .(415) 705-5555
Cliff House Visitor Center . . . .(415) 556-8642
Fort Funston Visitor Center . . . .(415) 239-2366
Fort Point Visitor Center . . . .(415) 556-1693
GGNPA Headquarters, Fort Mason . . . .(415) 561-3000
GGNRA Headquarters, Fort Mason . . . .(415) 556-0560
Lost and Found . . . .(415) 561-5107
Pacifica Visitor Center . . . .(650) 355-4122
Police, fire, ambulance emergency 911
Presidio Visitor Center . . . .(415) 561-4323
TDD (telecommunications device for the deaf) . . . . .(415) 556-2766

NEIGHBORING PARKS AND FACILITIES
Angel Island State Park . . . .(415) 435-1915
Bay Area Discovery Museum . . . .(415) 289-7268
The Exploratorium . . . . (415) 561-0360/563-7337
Farallones National Marine Sanctuary . . . .(415) 561-6622
Headlands Center for the Arts . . . .(415) 331-2787
Historical Park (Hyde Street Pier) . . . .(415) 556-3002/556-6435
John Muir National Historic Site, Martinez . . . .(510) 228-8860
Marine Mammal Center . . . .(415) 289-7325
Marin County Open Space District . . . .(415) 499-6387
National Maritime Museum, San Francisco . . . .(415) 556-3002
San Francisco Maritime National Slide
    Ranch Environmental Education . . . .(415) 381-6155

OTHER RESOURCES
Anne Kent California History Room . . . .(415) 499-7419
Jack Mason History Museum, Inverness . . . .(415) 669-1099
Marin County Historical Society . . . .(415) 454-8538
Mount Tamalpais
    History Project . . . . .22 South Green, Larkspur, CA 94939
Tamalpais Conservation Club . . . .(415) 391-8021

TRANSPORTATION
CalTrans road information . . . .(800) 427-7623
Golden Gate Transit . . . .(415) 921-5858
Gray Line Bus Service . . . .(800) 826-0202
Mill Valley Taxi . . . .(415) 383-8484

Sausalito Taxi . . . .(415) 332-2200

VISITOR SERVICES

Marin County Visitors Bureau . . . .(415) 472-7470
Mill Valley Chamber of Commerce . . . .(415) 388-9700
Point Reyes Station Chamber of Commerce . . . .(415) 663-9232
San Francisco Chamber of Commerce . . . .(415) 392-4520
San Francisco Convention and Visitors Bureau . . . . .(415) 391-2000
Sausalito Chamber of Commerce . . . .(415) 331-7262
Stinson Beach Chamber of Commerce . . . .(415) 868-1444

TRANSPORTATION & TOUR COMPANIES

These companies are registered to serve Muir Woods.

NAME	CITY	PHONE
Adventure U.S.A.	San Francisco, CA	(415) 441-0310
All West Coach Lines, Inc.	Sacramento, CA	(916) 423-4000
Antelope Valley Bus, Inc.	Lancaster, CA	(805) 948-8421
Arrow Stage Lines, Inc.	Phoenix, AZ	(602) 437-3484
Associated Limousines, Inc.	San Francisco, CA	(415) 563-1000
Bauer's Limousine	San Francisco, CA	(415) 522-1212
Cable Car Charters, Inc.	San Francisco, CA	(415) 922-2425
California Charter Service	Long Beach, CA	(562) 634-7969
Champagne Coaches, Inc.	San Leandro, CA	(510) 613-1136
CJSL Inc., Super Sightseeing	San Francisco, CA	(415) 777-2288
Coach 21	Daly City, CA	(415) 584-7271
Compass Transportation, Inc.	San Francisco, CA	(415) 641-3104
A Day in Nature	San Francisco, CA	(415) 673-0548
Day Tripping	Santa Rosa, CA	(707) 577-8894
Destination Systems	South San Francisco, CA	(650) 827-1000
Eastshore Charter Lines	Richmond, CA	(510) 451-9042
Ernie's Tour U.S.A., Inc.	South San Francisco, CA	(605) 588-8878
Evans, Inc.	Napa, CA	(707) 255-1557
Exel Charter Lines, Inc.	San Francisco, CA	(415) 666-0766
Franciscan Lines, Inc.	San Francisco, CA	(415) 642-9400
Golden Bay Transportation	San Francisco, CA	(415) 824-4653
Golden City Tours, Inc.	Millbrae, CA	(650) 692-3044
Great American Stage	Orangevale, CA	(916) 929-8833
Green Tortoise	San Francisco, CA	(415) 956-7500
Grosvenor Bus Lines	San Francisco, CA	(415) 558-7300
Lorrie's Travels and Tours	South San Francisco, CA	(415) 334-9000
Marin Charter and Tours	San Rafael, CA	(415) 256-8833
MDM Limousine and Sedan Service	San Francisco, CA	(415) 929-7000
Mercury Tours	South San Francisco, CA	(650) 588-1448
Music Express San Francisco, Inc.	Burlingame, CA	(415) 357-5054
Okabe International, Inc.	San Francisco, CA	(415) 921-0146
Orange Belt Stages	Visalia, CA	(209) 733-4408
Pacific Coast Bus Service, Inc.	San Francisco, CA	(415) 284-1600
Pacific Explorer Lines, Inc.	San Francisco, CA	(415) 641-3870
Portofino Tour Services	San Francisco, CA	(415) 777-9167
Royal Coach Tours	San Jose, CA	(408) 279-4801
Royal Livery Management	San Francisco, CA	(415) 431-1993
San Francisco/Petaluma KOA	Petaluma, CA	(707) 763-1492

These companies are registered to serve Muir Woods.

San Francisco/San Mateo Minibus	San Francisco, CA	(415) 777-5556
Save and Save Travel	San Francisco, CA	(415) 291-0879
Scenic Hyway Tours, Inc.	San Francisco, CA	(415) 647-1400
Serendipity Land Yachts, Ltd.	Santa Clara, CA	(408) 566-0430
Shangrila Express, Inc.	San Francisco, CA	(415) 956-9240
Sierra Pacific Tours	Concord, CA	(925) 825-8500
Thunderstar Stages	Petaluma, CA	(707) 778-3817
Tour Transport, Inc.	San Francisco, CA	(415) 626-7007
The Transportation Co.	South San Francisco, CA	(800) 869-4644
West Coast Limousine and Transportation	San Francisco, CA	(415) 864-7644

What is the elevation of Muir Woods?
The main parking lot is 150 feet above sea level.

Does Muir Woods have the tallest redwood in the world?
No. The tallest redwood tree in the world measures 367.8 feet and is located in Redwood National Park in Northern California The coast redwoods in Muir Woods are examples of the tallest species of redwoods, with our tallest one, in Bohemian Grove, measuring 253 feet.

Where is the drive-through tree?
The one most people remember is the Wawona Tree, a giant sequoia in Yosemite National Park that toppled over during the winter of 1969 from the weight of a heavy snow. We know of another drive-through tree—a coast redwood on privately owned land 150 miles north of Muir Woods on Highway 101 in Leggett, California.

Where is the walk-through tree?
The so-called walk-through tree in Muir Woods was in Cathedral Grove, but it fell in December 1971. After living for about 600 years, it couldn't survive the cumulative effects of unrestricted trampling around its base. We have since installed a fence to prevent this from happening to the surviving redwoods in Cathedral Grove.

Does the lichen hurt the trees?
Lichen does not harm trees. It's composed of two organisms—an alga and a fungus—that live together. The fungus is the body of the lichen, while the alga supplies the food through photosynthesis. Lichen thrives in damp, clean air; that's why it grows profusely in Muir Woods. It doesn't grow on the redwoods because the tannin in redwood bark inhibits the growth of any fungus.

How much wood is in a redwood tree?
Individual redwoods have been known to produce 100,000–200,000 board feet of lumber. One tree was reported to have produced 361,000 board feet of lumber—enough to build thirty or more homes. The Church of One Tree in Santa Rosa, California, which holds 500 people, was constructed from a single redwood tree. Normal yields from one acre of redwoods range from 35,000 to 100,000 board feet.

Why do some of the trees have even rows of holes in them?
Those holes are made by the yellow-bellied sapsucker, a member of the woodpecker family. It drills the holes, mostly in bay trees, to drink sap and trap insects.

How fast do coast redwood trees grow?
Several authorities say that, after a redwood reaches maturity
(approximately 100 years), the tree gains 1 inch of radius every sev-
enteen years. Young, healthy redwoods growing under ideal conditions, can gain up to 12 inches in height per year. The growth rate of
any tree is determined by rainfall, exposure, soil compaction, density,
and a host of other factors.

Where are the tallest trees in Muir Woods?
Our tallest redwoods, measuring over 250 feet tall, are located in
Bohemian Grove (a ten-minute walk up the trail), and Cathedral
Grove (a fifteen-minute walk up the trail).

*What are the trees on the way into Muir Woods that are shedding
their bark?*
Eucalyptus trees—imported from Australia nearly 100 years ago.

What word associated with redwood trees has all five vowels?
Sequoia.

Who has the most things named after him in the United States?
John Muir.

Which state has two state trees?
California: the coast redwood and the giant sequoia.

What gastropod often seen in Muir Woods is named after a fruit?
The banana slug. Look for this bright yellow animal in the moist and
cool environments of the woods.

*What animal seen annually in Muir Woods can live in both fresh
and salt water?*
The salmon.

Which leaf is noted for its aroma along the Muir Woods trails?
The California bay, or laurel (*Umbellularia californica*). It's often used
as a cooking spice.

What is the largest native mammal in Muir Woods?
The black-tailed mule deer, which descends into Redwood Canyon in
late spring to give birth. Antlered bucks can be seen in the late summer and fall in the woods.

What makes a redwood red?
Tannin. This chemical also helps redwoods resist damage from fungi,
insects, and fires.

Did I see an oriole in the woods on my winter walk?

Frequently mistaken for an oriole or robin, the varied thrush is a common winter resident of Muir Woods. It has an orange breast with a band of gray or black across it. It lives on the floors of coniferous forests, where it feeds on worms and insects. It also has a distinctive quavering song.

Will I see a rainbow trout in Redwood Creek?

You probably will. Redwood Creek is a free-flowing coastal creek that hosts both rainbow trout, in its freshwater pools, and steelhead trout, which swim in from the ocean to spawn and spend time in the creek's riffles. Although most rainbows spend their whole lives in freshwater, some also migrate with steelhead to the ocean.

Three programs in and around Muir Woods involve volunteers in various ways to educate the public and help preserve and restore the natural resources. Each concentrates on one area: Muir Woods National Monument, Mount Tamalpais State Park, or the Marin Municipal Water District lands.

MUIR WOODS NATIONAL MONUMENT

The Golden Gate National Parks Association (GGNPA) is a nonprofit membership organization established to support the education, conservation, and research programs of the Golden Gate National Recreation Area. The association offers numerous opportunities for volunteers to help preserve, protect, and restore the natural resources of Muir Woods and the Redwood Creek watershed. The GGNPA volunteer programs in Muir Woods are coordinated by GGNRA resource managers at the Muir Woods Nursery and by interpretive rangers.

Volunteer workdays in the field are every Wednesday and Sunday, from 10 a.m. to 1 p.m. Participants meet at the Muir Woods Nursery, located on the lower Muir Woods Road, just past the last parking lot. Volunteer training is conducted by GGNRA resource staff, and projects take place primarily on National Park Service lands, with some work on state parklands. You can also participate in one of the Earth Day events in Muir Woods; one is in January and the other in April. To be part of the interpretive staff at Muir Woods, you need to volunteer for 10 hours a month and undergo training conducted by GGNRA rangers and other experienced park service volunteers.

For more information on volunteer programs in Muir Woods and the Redwood Creek watershed, contact Heather King at (415) 388-3267, the visitor center at (415) 388-2596, or the GGNRA volunteer hotline at (415) 561-4325. To join the GGNPA, see the membership application on page 106.

Here's a sampling of some GGNPA volunteer projects:

- **Serving as an interpretive ranger.** Volunteers staff the information table in front of the visitor center, rove trails to answer visitors' questions, and prepare and present interpretive programs for the public.

- **Working in the Muir Woods Nursery:** Volunteers work on propagating native plant species that can grow in a variety of habitats or help with construction and other projects.

- **Replanting native species and doing erosion-control work:** Volunteers clear, plant, and protect identified areas that have been damaged through natural erosion, development, or agricultural activities.

- **Restoring native habitats:** This work consists of a variety of tasks to restore areas that have been eroded or otherwise disturbed. Some ongoing projects involve the understory of Muir Woods, the Redwood Creek habitat, songbird nesting habitats, the Muir Beach dunes, the old Golden Gate Dairy, and the flood plains and wetlands of the lower Redwood Creek watershed.

- **Controlling the spread of non-native trees and plants:** Work parties are sent to identified areas to clear invasive, non-native plants such as Scotch broom. Other tasks include mapping exotic species within the watershed.

- **Counting and monitoring endangered or threatened wildlife species:** This work currently includes counting coho salmon during the winter spawning run, searching the wetlands around Muir Beach at night for the red-legged frog, and monitoring the nighttime activities of the northern spotted owl in Muir Woods.

MOUNT TAMALPAIS STATE PARK

The Mount Tamalpais Interpretative Association (MTIA) is a volunteer membership organization that promotes conservation of, education about, and interpretation of lands primarily in Mount Tamalpais State Park. Association members are knowledgeable about the history, geology, and ecology of Mount Tam, and many volunteer 40 hours or more each year to help the park disseminate this information to the public. For more details, contact the association office at (415) 258-2410; for membership information, call (415) 924-7887 (a membership application can be found on page 107.)

Here's a sampling of MTIA volunteer projects:

- **Working at the East Peak Visitor Center on Mount Tam.** Volunteers answer questions and distribute information to visitors about the many resources of the state park. Weekends only; visitor center hours vary according to the season.

- **Leading interpretive hikes for the public.** The association sponsors hikes for the public on Saturdays and Sundays throughout the year. These hikes focus on a variety of subjects, including mushrooms, wildflowers, fire ecology, Tam trivia, and Tam history. MTIA also offers special hikes on New Year's Day and during full moons.

- **Producing, distributing, and selling interpretive and educational materials.** The association produces and distributes materials that help visitors interpret the many aspects of the Mount Tam area.

- **Helping the state park conserve and interpret areas of historic and cultural interest.** The association has assisted in the construction of a Gravity Car Barn at East Peak, which will feature historic displays and programs about the Mount Tamalpais and Muir Woods Railway. The group also maintains extensive files on the natural resources, history, and cultural features of Mount Tamalpais.

- **Fundraising to support programs of the state park.** Fundraising events include sales of merchandise, special interpretive hikes for private groups, presentations to community groups, hike-a-thons, and membership parties.

MARIN MUNICIPAL WATER DISTRICT LANDS

The Marin Municipal Water District (MMWD) controls the largest amount of land on Mount Tamalpais, including most of the north side and a large area from West Point Inn to Mountain Home Inn. To help preserve and maintain these lands, MMWD has an active volunteer program, which engages in a variety of land management activities. For more information about the program, contact the volunteer coordinator at the Sky Oaks Ranger Station, (415) 459-5267.

Here's a sampling of MMWD volunteer projects:

- **Habitat restoration.** Volunteers are trained to work in groups one Saturday each month to remove French broom and Scotch broom from the Mount Tamalpais watershed. Participants receive a "Broom Busters" certificate, which enables them to remove broom anytime, anywhere on Mount Tamalpais.

- **Natural resource mapping.** Volunteers learn to use Global Positioning System equipment to map facilities, structures, flora, and fauna in the Mount Tamalpais watershed. By entering this information into the MMWD Geographical Information Computer System (GIS), volunteers see how the various features of the watershed are analyzed and monitored.

- **Adopt-a-Lake program.** Individual volunteers or private and corporate groups can choose a lake in the watershed and perform ongoing maintenance by removing non-native plants and cleaning debris from shorelines.

- **Visitor assistance.** Volunteers at the watershed entrance station answer questions, sell passes, and sell maps.

- **Mounted volunteers.** Volunteers who have horses ride the trails, providing information and first aid to visitors.

- **Adopt-a-Trail program.** Trail volunteers learn to install and maintain water bars, repair trail treads, control erosion, and build trail structures.

- **Office organization.** Volunteers assist the watershed management staff with computer work as well as other office activities and services.

- **Habitat study.** Volunteers assist in field studies to identify birds and plants, including monitoring rare habitats or collecting data for permanent vegetation plots and rare plant surveys.

- **Public education and outreach.** Volunteers give presentations at schools and community centers on the subjects of Mount Tamalpais history, geology, and wildlife.

- **Volunteer rangers.** Under supervision, volunteers assist state park rangers with patrol and maintenance of the watershed, including conducting talks and tours of watershed lands and maintaining and improving watershed signs, roads, trails, and recreation areas.

Further Reading

Adopt-a-Stream Foundation Field Guide to the Pacific Salmon by Robert Steelquist. Seattle, WA: Sasquatch Books, 1992.

All the Rain Promises and More: A Hip Pocket Guide to Western Mushrooms by David Arora. Santa Cruz, CA: BioSystems Books; Berkeley, CA: Ten Speed Press, 1991.

California's Wild Heritage: Threatened and Endangered Animals in the Golden State by Peter Steinhart. San Francisco: California Department of Fish and Game, California Academy of Sciences, Sierra Club Books, 1990.

A Civil History of Golden Gate National Recreation Area and Point Reyes National Seashore, volume I, by Anna Coxe Toogood. Denver: Historic Preservation Branch, Pacific Northwest/Western Team, Denver Service Center, National Park Service, U.S. Department of the Interior, 1980.

Coast Redwoods Nature Guide: An Easy Visual Key to Over 100 Common Animals, Birds and Plants of California's Coast Redwoods by Larry Eifert and Nancy Cherry Martin. 1998. Pamphlet sold at Muir Woods visitor center.

Erickson's Mount Tamalpais Trail Map by Eureka Cartography. Berkeley, CA: Eureka Cartography, 1991.

Golden Gate National Recreation Area Park Guide by Ariel Rubissow. San Francisco: Golden Gate National Parks Association, 1995 (reprinted).

An Island Called California: An Ecological Introduction to Its Natural Communities, 2nd edition, by Elna Bakker. Berkeley: University of California Press, 1984.

The Life of an Oak: An Intimate Portrait by Glenn Keator, artwork by Susan Bazell. Berkeley, CA: Heyday Books; Oakland, CA: California Oak Foundation, 1998.

Mill Valley: The Early Years by Barry Spitz in association with the Mill Valley Historical Society. Mill Valley, CA: Potrero Meadow Publishing Co., 1997.

The Monarch Habitat Handbook: A California Landowner's Guide to Managing Monarch Butterfly Overwintering Habitat by Lincoln P. Brower, Mia Monroe, and Katrin Snow. Portland, OR: Xerxes Society, 1997.

Mount Tamalpais: A History by Lincoln Fairley, picture editor James Heig. San Francisco: Scottwall Associates, 1987.

Mt. Tam: A Hiking, Running and Nature Guide, 2nd edition, by Don and Kay Martin. San Anselmo, CA: Martin Press, 1994.

Muir Woods: The Ancient Redwood Forest near San Francisco, revised edition, by James M. Morley. San Francisco: Smith-Morley, 1991.

Muir Woods: Map and Guide to Trails, Plants and Wildlife by the Golden Gate National Parks Association. San Francisco: Golden Gate National Parks Association, 1991.

Muir Woods, Redwood Refuge by John Hart. San Francisco: Golden Gate National Parks Association, 1991.

Plants of the Coast Redwood Region by Kathleen Lyons and Mary Beth Cooney-Lazaneo. Boulder Creek, CA: Looking Press, 1988.

A Rambler's Guide to the Trails of Mt. Tamalpais and the Marin Headlands: Complete Guide to Hiking, Biking, Horse Trails by Gerald W. Olmsted in association with the Mount Tamalpais History Project. Berkeley, CA: Olmsted & Bros. Map Co., 1998.

Tamalpais Trails, 4th edition, by Dewey Livingston, Barry Spitz, and Brad Rippe. Mill Valley, CA: Potrero Meadow Publishing Co., 1998.

Web of Water: Life in Redwood Creek by Maya Khosla. San Francisco: Golden Gate National Parks Association, 1997.

The Wilderness World of John Muir edited by Edwin Way Teale. Boston: Houghton Mifflin Co., 1982.

Alan P. Sieroty Beach, 79, 90

Albino redwood sprouts, 34

Alder, red, 28, 53

Alice Eastwood Camp, 68, 77, 108

Alice Eastwood Trail, 108

Alpine Lake, 61, 73, 108

Alpine Trail, 68

Amphibians, 41, 43

Aquatic wildlife, 36, 38–39, 43

Aralia, California (elk clover), 49, 52, 53

Aramark Corporation, 11, 114

Audubon Canyon Ranch, 48, 116

Automobiles, 4, 100, 101

Autumn visits, 6, 53, 57

Azalea, western, 49, 52

Backpacking camps, 75–76, 114

Banana slugs, 33, 41, 123

Bats, 33, 41, 43, 50

Battery Alexander Group Camp, 76

Bay-laurel, 28, 123

Beaches, 61, 78–79

Bear Valley Visitor Center, 48, 79, 90, 117

Bears, 40, 45

Ben Johnson Cabin, 99, 100, 108

Ben Johnson Trail, 19, 56, 62, 108
    ranger-led hikes on, 65
    suggested routes, 69, 70

Berries, 52

Bicentennial Camp, 76

Bicentennial Tree, 32

Bicycling, 4, 60–61, 71

Binoculars, 16, 42

Bird Island, 46

Birds, 40–41, 124
    aquatic, 39
    sounds of, 33, 42
    viewing, 42–43, 46–48

Boardwalk, 103

Bobcat Trail, 75

Bobcats, 40, 42, 65

Bohemian Club, 99, 108

Bolinas Lagoon, 47, 48

Bon Tempe Lake, 61, 73

Book recommendations, 129–30

Bookstore, 9, 11, 19, 20, 58

Bootjack Camp, 108

Bootjack Picnic Area, 89

Bootjack Trail, 43, 68, 69, 108

Bracken ferns, 49

Buckeye, California, 29, 51, 52, 53

Bufano, Benny, 103

Bus tours, 4, 103, 120–21

Bus transportation, 115, 118, 120–21

Bushtits, 40, 43

Butterflies, monarch, 53, 66, 94

Café, 9, 11, 85

California Alpine Club, 63

Camp Alice Eastwood, 68, 77, 108

Camp Alice Eastwood Grade, 66

Camping, 12–13, 14, 61, 74–77
  backpack camps, 75–76
  equipment and supplies, 98
  group camps, 76–77
  with horses, 72
  telephone directory, 114

Canoeing, 61

Cascades, 38, 74

Cataract Trail, 70

Cathedral Grove, 21, 57, 68, 103, 108, 109

Chambers of commerce, 119

Chaparral, 55

Children, 19, 20, 68, 69

Chipmunks, Sonoma, 41, 43, 44, 45

Civilian Conservation Corps, 102, 108, 111, 112

Clifftop Trail, 46

Climate, 6, 16, 30-31

Clothing, 16, 67, 98

Clothing-optional beaches, 78, 90

Clover, elk (California aralia), 49, 52, 53

Coast Miwok people, 22

Coastal Trail, 109
  ranger-led hikes on, 65
  suggested route, 70
  wildflowers, 52

Concrete Bridge, 109

Conlon Road, 109

Controlled burns, 50, 103

Cost of entry, 7

Coyote Ridge Trail, 70, 76

Coyotes, 40, 42, 45

Crayfish, 38, 39, 53, 103

Creepers, brown, 40, 43

Cross, Andrew Jay, 32

Crowds, avoiding, 56

Dan Sealy's Pool, 38, 109

Deer, 28, 33, 40, 42, 123

Deer Park Ridge Trail, 65

Deer Park Trail, 62, 66

Dias Ridge, 109

Dias Ridge Trail, 65

Dining facilities, 9, 85–88
  directory, 115–16
  hiking to, 91, 116

Dipsea Race, 100, 109

Dipsea Trail, 19, 55, 62, 65, 66, 109
  suggested routes, 70

Disabled, access for
  campsite, 75-76
  picnic areas, 89

Distances to Muir Woods, 3

Dogs, 14–15

Douglas fir, 29, 32, 55

Dragonflies, 39

Drakes Beach, 79

Driving to Muir Woods, 4, 5

Druid Ridge, 109

Ducks, 40, 43, 46, 47

Earth Day (January), 93, 117
Earthquake and Fire of 1906, 23, 100
East Peak, 109
Eastwood, Alice, 108
Easy Grade Trail, 68
Educational fee waivers, 117
Educational programs, 104–5, 114
Egrets, 46, 47, 48
Eldridge Grade, 109
Elevation, 122
Elk, 40
Elk clover (California aralia), 49, 52, 53
Emerson, Ralph Waldo, 32
Entrance fees, 7
Environmental planning, 95
Equipment and supplies, 67, 98
Eucalyptus, 123

Fall color, 53, 57
Fall visits, 6, 53
Family circles, 34
Fees, 7, 103, 117
Fern Creek Bridge, 102
Fern Creek Trail, 62
    for avoiding crowds, 56
    Kent tree on, 32
    ranger-led hikes, 65
    suggested routes, 55, 68, 69
    wildlife on, 43
Ferns, 49. See also Horsetail ferns

Ferry tours, 4
Filberts. See Hazelnuts
Fire facts, 50, 101, 102, 103
Fire safety, 64
Fishing, 61, 73
Five Brooks Ranch and Stables, 72, 117
Flowers, 51–52
Foxes, gray, 40, 42
Frank's Valley, 66
Frank's Valley Group Horse Camp, 72, 77
Fungi, 41, 49, 64
Future of Muir Woods, 95

Geological history, 22
Getting to Muir Woods, 4–5
GGNPA. See Golden Gate National Parks Association
GGNRA. See Golden Gate National Recreation Area
Giardiasis, 36, 64
Gift shop, 9, 11, 58
Glen Camp, 76
Golden Access Pass, 7
Golden Age Pass, 7
Golden Eagle Pass, 7
Golden Gate Bridge, 102
Golden Gate Dairy, 110
Golden Gate Hostel, 84, 115
Golden Gate National Parks Association (GGNPA), 11, 114
    membership application, 106
    programs, 113, 117, 125-26

Golden Gate National Recreation Area (GGNRA), 2, 60-61, 71, 72
    beaches, 78–79
    birdwatching, 47, 48
    camping, 13, 74–77
    directory, 118
    volunteer hotline, 117
Golden Gate Raptor Observatory, 46, 116
Gravity Car Grade, 25, 68, 110
Green Gulch Farm Zen Center, 92, 94, 110
Green Gulch Guest House, 91, 92, 116
Green Gulch Trail, 70
Group campgrounds, 76–77

Hagmaeir Pond, 90
Hawk Backpack Camp, 75
Hawk Hill, 46, 110
Hawks, Cooper's, 41, 43, 46
Hawkwatch Hotline, 46, 116
Haypress Backpack Camp, 75–76
Hazelnuts, 49, 52
Heart's Desire Beach, 79, 90
Helen Markt Trail, 70
Herons, great blue, 39, 40, 43, 45, 47, 48, 103
Hidden Lake Trail, 110
High Marsh Trail, 70
Hiking, 18–21, 60, 62–64
    avoiding crowds, 56
    equipment and supplies, 67, 98

interpretive walks, 19, 20, 65–66, 116, 117
    ocean views, 55
    suggested routes, 68–70
    to dining and lodging, 91–92, 116
    to Muir Woods, 5
Hillside Trail, 19, 21, 62, 68
History, 22–27, 99–103
    of hiking trails, 63
    ranger talks on, 65, 66
Hogback Trail, 68, 69
Holiday Inn Express, 83, 115
Homestead Valley, 110
Horseback camping, 72, 77
Horseback riding, 60–61, 72
Horsetail ferns, 41, 43, 49, 53, 110
Hostels, 84, 115
Hotels. See Lodging
Hours, 8
Huckleberries, 40, 49, 52

Inns. See Lodging
Insects, 38, 39, 63
Interpretive walks, 19, 20, 65–66, 116, 117

Jays, scrub, 41, 43
Jays, Steller's, 33, 40, 42, 45

Kayaking, 61
Kent, William, 23, 26, 27, 32, 99, 100, 101
Kent Canyon, 65

Kent Lake, 61, 73, 110

Kent Trail, 70, 110

Kent Tree, 32, 101

Khosla, Maya, 39, 130

Kirby Cove, 61

Kirby Cove Group Camp, 76–77

Ladybugs, 41, 43, 53, 110

Lagunitas Creek, 116

Lagunitas, Lake, 61, 73

Lakes, 61, 73

Land grant, 23, 99

Laurel, bay, 28, 123

Laurel Dell, 110

Lichens, 40, 49, 122

Limantour Beach, 79, 84

Lind, Andrew, 101

Lizards, 41, 43

Lodging, 9, 12, 82–84

  directory, 115

  hiking to, 91–92

Logging, 23, 99

Lone Tree Spring, 65

Lost Trail, 55, 69, 110

Lyme disease, 63

Madrone, 55

Main Loop Trail, 21, 55, 62

  crowds on, 56

  curly bark redwood on, 34

  suggested hikes, 68–70

Maple Meadow, 110

Maples, big-leaf, 28, 53

Maps, 10, 88

  campgrounds, 77

  dog-friendly trails, 15

  driving to Muir Woods, 5

  lodging, 92

  Marin County, 13

  watershed, 37

Marin Bicycle Trails Council, 71, 117

Marin County Historical Society, 118

Marin County Visitors Bureau, 119

Marin Headlands

  beaches, 78

  birdwatching, 46

  camping, 75, 76–77

  hiking, 66, 117

  hostel, 84

  picnic areas, 89, 116

  Visitor Center, 46, 72, 116

  wildflowers, 52

Marin Municipal Water District

  fishing, 73, 117

  trails, 72, 108

  volunteer programs, 117, 127–28

Marincello Trail, 75

Matt Davis Trail, 69, 70, 111

Mementos, 58

Migration hike, 66

Mill Valley

  Chamber of Commerce, 119

  dining, 87, 115

  lodging, 83, 115

Mill Valley and Mount Tamalpais Scenic Railway, 99, 100

Millerton Point, 79, 90

Miwok Livery Stables, 72, 117

Miwok people, 22

Miwok Trail, 65

backpack camp route, 75

hiking route, 70

wildflowers, 52

Moles, 41, 43

Monarch butterflies, 53, 66, 94

Morley, James M., 57, 130

Mosses, 49

Mount Tamalpais

camping, 74, 77

lodging, 82

mountain biking, 71

picnic areas, 89, 116

plant life, 55

Mount Tamalpais History Project, 118

Mount Tamalpais Interpretive Association, 66

hiking information, 117

membership application, 107

Mount Tamalpais and Muir Woods Railway, 23, 24–25

Mount Tamalpais State Park, 2, 101

camping, 12–13, 74, 77

contacting, 72

educational programs, 105

volunteer programs, 117, 126–27

Mountain biking 4, 60–61, 71

Mountain Home Inn, 12, 66, 92, 111, 115

dining, 86

hiking routes from, 68, 69

hiking to, 91

lodging, 82

Mountain lions, 33, 40, 42

first sitings of, 102

safety concerns, 45, 63

Mountain Theater, 89, 102, 105

Muir, John, 26, 27, 100, 101, 108, 123

Muir Beach, 61, 65, 78, 111

camping, 75–76

dining, 86

hiking to, 68

lodging, 82, 115

monarch butterflies at, 94

picnic areas, 89–90, 116

summer solstice at, 93

Muir Inn, 100, 101, 108

Muir Woods Nursery, 116, 125

Muir Woods Ranger Station, 50, 90, 117

Muir Woods Road, hiking on, 68, 70

Muir Woods: The Ancient Redwood Forest near San Francisco (Morley), 57, 130

Muir Woods Trail, 62

Museums, 118

Mushrooms. See Fungi

Name plaques on trees, 32

National monument status, 2, 23,
80, 100

National Park Service (NPS), 11, 114, 117

Native Americans, 22

Nettles, stinging, 54

Newts, California, 41, 43

Nora Trail, 69

NPS. *See* National Park Service

Nude beaches, 78, 90

Nursery, 116, 125

Oak, poison, 53, 54, 63–64

Oaks, 52

Oaks, tanbark, 28, 29, 53, 55

Ocean View Trail, 55, 62, 111
  suggested route, 69
  Tourist Club, 91
  wildflowers on, 52

Old Inn, 111

Old Mine Trail, 69

Old Railroad Grade, 68, 69

Old Stage Road, 68, 69

Olema Creek, 116

Olema Ranch Campground, 75

Olema Valley, picnic areas, 90

O'Rourke's Bench, 111

Owls, 33, 41, 43

Oxalis, 42, 49, 51

Pacific Flyway, 66. *See also* Birds

Pan Toll, 111
  camping, 74
  hiking routes, 69, 70
  lodging, 91
  picnic area, 89

Pan Toll Ranger Station, 72

Panoramic Trail. *See* Ocean View Trail

Park rangers. *See* Rangers

"Parkitecture," 102

Pelican Inn, 12, 82, 92, 115
  hiking to, 91

Phoenix Lake, 61, 73

Photography hints, 57, 58

Picnicking, 9, 14, 89–90, 116

Pinchot, Gifford, 23, 100, 101, 108

Pinchot tree, 32, 34

Planning for the future, 95

Plant life, 49–54
  flowers, 51–52
  poisonous, 53, 54, 63 64
  prescribed burns and, 50

Point Reyes Hostel, 84, 115

Point Reyes National Seashore, 61, 116
  beaches, 79
  birdwatching, 48
  camping, 13, 75, 76, 79
  dining, 86
  hiking information, 66, 117
  horseback riding, 72
  lodging, 82, 84, 91, 92, 115, 116, 117
  picnic areas, 90, 116

Point Reyes Station Chamber of Commerce, 119

Poison oak, 53, 54, 63–64, 67

Prescribed burns, 50, 103

Quail, 41, 43

Quietness, 33

Raccoons, 40, 42

Railway, 24–25, 99, 100, 102

Rainy-season visits, 6, 16, 39

A Rambler's Guide to the Trails of Mt. Tamalpais and the Marin Headlands, 62, 130

Rancho Sausalito, 23, 99

Ranger Mia, contacting, 96

Ranger Station, 50, 90, 117

Rangers, 11
    checking trail conditions with, 62
    interpretive walks with, 19, 20, 116, 117

Raptors, 46, 65, 66, 110, 116

Rats, wood, 41, 43

Rattlesnakes, 63

Ravens, 33, 40, 42

Reading suggestions, 129–30

Red Rock Beach, 78

Redwood Canyon acquisition, 23, 100

Redwood Creek
    plant life, 52, 53
    water quality, 36
    watershed, 36, 37

    wildlife, 36, 38–39, 41, 42, 43, 116

Redwood Creek Trail
    for avoiding crowds, 56
    ranger-led hikes, 65, 66
    suggested routes, 68, 70

Redwood Trail, ocean-viewing route, 55

Redwoods, 34–35
    age of, 22, 23, 30, 35
    drive- or walk-through, 122
    fall changes in, 53
    leaves, 29
    lumber yields, 122
    name plaques on, 32
    prescribed burns and, 50
    size of, 30–31, 122, 123
    trivia about, 122–23, 124

Reptiles, 41

Reservations, 114

Restaurants. *See* Dining facilities

Restrooms, 9, 67

Richardson, William, 23, 99

Road condition reports, 117, 118

Rock Spring Trail, 69, 111

Rocky Point, camping, 74

Rodeo Beach, 46, 61, 78, 89

Rodeo Lagoon, 46, 89

Rodeo Valley, 46, 84

Roosevelt, Franklin Delano, 32, 102

Roosevelt, Theodore, 23, 26, 100

Safety concerns

falling branches, 54
hiking and, 63–64
poisonous plants, 54
water, 36, 64
wildlife, 45, 63
Salamanders, 41, 43
Salmon, 33, 36, 38, 39, 41, 43, 66
as fresh or saltwater fish, 123
restoration project, 117
spawning information, 116
Samuel P. Taylor State Park, 75, 90, 116
San Francisco Chamber of Commerce, 119
San Francisco Convention and Visitors Bureau, 119
Santos Meadow, 72, 111
Sausalito
Chamber of Commerce, 119
dining, 87–88, 115–16
lodging, 83–84, 115
School transportation, 105, 114, 117
Scrub jays, 41, 43
Seasonal variations, 6
in crowds, 56
fall color, 53
photography hints, 57, 58
in plant life, 49, 51–52
special events, 93, 117
in wildlife, 39, 41, 43, 45, 94
Seed cones, 35
Self-guiding nature trail, 9
Seniors, entry free for, 7

Sequoia Canyon acquisition, 23, 100
Sequoia sempervirens. See Redwoods
Shorebirds, 46, 47, 48
Sierra Club, hiking with, 63
Skunks, 40
Slide Ranch, 61
Slugs, banana, 33, 41, 123
Snakes, 41, 63
Souvenirs, 58
Spanish occupation, 22–23
Spitz, Barry, 62, 130
Springtime visits, 6
Sprouts, 34
Squirrels, 28, 33, 41, 43, 44, 102, 103
Stapelveldt Trail, 62, 70, 111
Steelhead. *See* Trout
Steep Ravine Environmental Campground, 74
Steep Ravine Trail, 70, 74, 111
Steller's jays, 33, 40, 42, 45
Stinson Beach, 61, 78, 112
camping, 74
Chamber of Commerce, 119
dining, 86–87, 116
hiking to, 70
lodging, 82, 115
picnic area, 90, 116
Ranger Station, 90, 117
surf and parking hotline, 117
Summer solstice events, 93, 117
Summertime visits, 6, 8, 16
Sun Trail, 52, 55, 112
Surfing, 61, 78

Swimming, 61, 78, 79

Tamalpais Conservation Club (TCC), 63, 118. *See also* TCC Trail
Tamalpais Trails (Spitz), 62, 130
Tanbark oak (tanoak), 28, 29, 53, 55
Taxis, 118
TCC Trail, 66, 69, 112
Telephone directory, 114–21
Telephones, 9
Tennessee Cove, 112
Tennessee Valley
    backpack camping from, 75–76
    horse stables, 72
    picnic areas, 89
    wildflowers, 52
Tennessee Valley Beach, 78
Terwilliger, Elizabeth, 94
Terwilliger Grove, 66
Thrushes, 40–41, 124
Ticks, 16, 63, 67
Tidepooling, 61, 65
Timing your visit, 6, 8, 21, 33
Toll road, 101
Tomales Bay wildlife sanctuary, 48
Tomales Bay State Park, 79, 90
    Ranger Station, 117
Tour buses, 4, 103, 120-21
Tour reservations, 114
Tourist Club, 55, 63, 91, 92, 112, 116

Trails, 18–21, 60, 62
    boardwalk, 103
    building of, 103
    condition reports, 117
    dog-friendly, 15
    horseback, 60-61, 72
    length of, 9, 21
    suggested routes, 68–70
Transportation, 4–5
    directory, 115, 118, 120–21
    railway, 24–25, 99, 100, 102
    for schools, 105, 114, 117
Trees, 28–29, 122-23. *See also specific kinds*
Trivia, 122–24
Troop 80 Trail, 66
Trout fishing, 73
Trout, rainbow, 38, 124
Trout, steelhead, 36, 38, 39, 41, 43, 66, 124
Turtles, western pond, 36, 38

United Nations tree, 32, 103

Van Wyck Meadow, 112
Violets, redwood, 51
Visiting hours, 8
Visitor center, 9, 11, 19, 20
    hiking routes from, 68–70
    mementos in, 58
    opening of, 103
Visitor services, 9, 119
Visitors, number of, 2

Voles, 40, 41, 43
Volunteers, 9, 19, 20, 93
  information for, 117
  programs, 125–28
Von Voss, Lee, 102

Walking. *See* Hiking; Trails
Warblers, 40–41, 47
Water, 16
  health concerns, 36, 64
Water recreation areas, 61
Waterfalls, 38, 74
Waterfowl, 48, 66
"Watershed council," 95
Weather, 6, 16
*Web of Water: Life in Redwood
  Creek* (Khosla), 39, 130
Webb Creek, 74
Wells, F. Marion, 99
West Peak, 112
West Point Inn, 91, 92, 112, 116
West Point Inn Association, 91
West Point Trail, 69
Whales, 60, 66
Wildcat Camp, 76
Wildfires, 50
Wildflowers, 51–52
Wildlife, 6, 18, 33, 40–48
  aquatic, 36, 38–39, 43
  dangers, 45
  feeding of prohibited, 44, 45
  migration hike, 66

plants to avoid, 54
trivia about, 123
viewing, 42–43, 44
See also specific kinds
Wind dangers, 54
Winter solstice events, 93, 117
Wintertime visits, 6, 16, 39
Wobbly Rock, 112
Wolf Ridge Trail, 52
Wood rats, 41, 43
Wrens, winter, 40, 42, 46

Yellow jackets, 63

Acknowledgments

We are indebted to Mia Monroe and Josh Englander for their invaluable help in developing and editing the manuscript; local historians Al Graves, Bill Provines, Fred Runner, Fred Sandrock and the Mount Tamalpais History Project, Barry Spitz, Jim Staley, and Ted Wurm for their generous assistance with research, historic resource materials, and/or editing; National Park Service historian Steve Haller for his review of the chronological information; photographer and author James M. Morley for his contributions on photography in the woods; Jane Arnold, Molly Schardt, the Bohemian Club Photo Archives, Good Buy Sweet Prints, and the National Maritime Park Photo Archives for their help in locating historic photos and documents; the National Park Service staff at the Golden Gate National Recreation Area, especially Brett Bankie and Chris Powell for their help in reviewing and editing the manuscript; Cathy Petrick at the Marin Headlands Visitor Center for her help with resource information; the Golden Gate National Parks Association, especially Susan Tasaki for her help with reprinted materials; Carolyn Shoulders of the National Park Service Natural Resources Office; Historian Nancy Skinner and Membership Director Sarah Davis of the Mount Tamalpais Interpretive Association; Cindy Fadin, Coordinator of Marin Municipal Water District Volunteer Programs; Anne Marie Bossardet of Aramark Corporation; Deborah Dallinger of Audubon Canyon Ranch; Sheila McBrien of the American Automobile Association; Janet Dean and Pam McCosker for their help in researching and producing the information; and the National Park Service staff at Muir Woods for their help in making this guidebook as accurate as possible.

Historic photos were obtained from the Golden Gate National Recreation Area Photo Collection; National Maritime Park Photo Archives; the Kent Family Collection; the Al Graves Collection; the Bohemian Club Photo Archives; the Mount Tamalpais History Project; and Good Buy Sweet Prints.

Thank you!

About the Author
Susan Frank spent many of her childhood weekends camping in the Sierra Nevada and fishing California rivers and lakes with her family. She saw her first grizzly bear on the Katmai Peninsula in Alaska at age ten and spent more enjoyable hours waiting for fish to bite her line than actually catching them. After earning a degree in European history from the University of California, Berkeley, she taught in Minnesota and California before starting a career in communications. In 1990 she founded a media and marketing consulting company, working with a variety of clients throughout the San Francisco Bay Area.

About the Illustrator
Cartoonist Phil Frank's daily cartoon strip, "Farley," has been keeping a finger on the pulse of the San Francisco Bay Area for more than ten years, ever since Phil decided to leave national syndication to focus his considerable talents on issues closer to home. The strip is dearly loved and followed daily by a local cadre of fans. Indeed, "Farley" has become one of San Francisco's most recognized and reliable landmarks.

Susan and Phil started their life together on a houseboat in Sausalito, California. This led to their first book collaboration, a children's book about living on the water. Both avid history buffs, they moved from ship to shore about ten years ago. At present they maintain a 1914 Craftsman-style home in Sausalito, from which they venture into the national parks and other wilderness areas in search of inspiration for new books. They have two grown children, two grandchildren, two Maltese-cross dogs, and two cats.